Positive Living

THE COMPLETE GUIDE TO
positive
thinking
AND
personal
success

VERA PEIFFER

PIATKUS

❧ *Visit the Piatkus website!*

Piatkus publishes a wide range of bestselling fiction and non-fiction, including books on health, mind, body & spirit, sex, self-help, cookery, biography and the paranormal.

If you want to:

- read descriptions of our popular titles
- buy our books over the internet
- take advantage of our special offers
- enter our monthly competition
- learn more about your favourite Piatkus authors

VISIT OUR WEBSITE AT: **www.piatkus.co.uk**

First published in 2001 by
Piatkus Books Limited
5 Windmill Street
London W1T 2JA
e-mail: info@piatkus.co.uk

Reprinted twice

This edition first published in 2005

The moral right of the author has been asserted

A catalogue record for this book is available from the British Library

ISBN 0 7499 2603 1

Text design Design 23
Edited by Matthew Cory

This book has been printed on paper manufactured with respect for the environment using wood from managed sustainable resources

Typeset by Palimpsest Book Production Limited,
Polmont, Stirlingshire
Printed and bound in Great Britain by
Mackays of Chatham Ltd

Positive Living

THE COMPLETE GUIDE TO
positive
thinking
AND
personal
success

For Carl, Laura and Christina,
with all my love

Contents

PART II: Solutions for Positive Living

Chapter Six: Work Life

Introduction

It is now over ten years ago that I wrote *Positive Thinking*. It is still a bestselling book, both in the United Kingdom and abroad. People from all over the world write to me saying that it helps them cope with problems and difficult life situations more constructively, releasing them from feelings of remorse, anger and hopelessness and helping them gain a positive outlook so they can find viable solutions.

However, a lot has changed in the world since the late 1980s. Technology has made giant strides forward, to an extent that few of us could have foreseen. Once, the person walking in the street with a personal stereo was considered a weird show-off. Back then a computer was a very expensive piece of technology which only large companies could afford to buy. Today, computers can be found in most homes, and children use them at least as often as adults. Technology has become simpler and more affordable and it has entirely changed the way we live and work. These changes are enriching, but they also speed up the pace of life. If you think about how you live now and then compare it with how busy you were five or ten years ago, you will probably find that your work schedule has become much more demanding. I know that my own workload, and other potential sources of stress, have been on the increase since I first started writing in the late eighties!

At my hypnotherapy and health kinesiology practice, I see more and more people who find it difficult to cope with the additional stresses that our present lifestyle brings, and this made me think that it would be helpful to look at these new sources of stress and explore how we can deal with them more efficiently.

There are times for most of us when we feel we are drowning in the demands made on us. I'm sure you could name at least three or four stresses in your life that make you feel overwhelmed at times. These demands come from your immediate environment such as employers, family and friends, but they also come from within yourself. Quite naturally, we want to prosper and we want to lead a fulfilling life, so we will make every effort to succeed. There is nothing wrong with that, but it is important that we make sure we do not spin into overdrive. If you feel that you are sometimes pushed to the edge of what you can handle or tolerate, it is time to take stock and do something about the pressures you are under.

I am very conscious through the work with my clients that the pressures on them are made worse by their growing awareness that stress is detrimental to their health. They are not only stressed by the multiple tasks of earning a living, looking after the children and keeping a household running, but they also feel they need to eat more healthily, stop smoking and cram an exercise class or a session with a relaxation tape into their already over-brimming schedule. And if they can't manage it, they feel guilty, which makes them feel even more stressed . . . I'm sure many of you are familiar with this vicious circle.

But this is not where the problems stop. The pace of change also brings with it a sense of dislocation. Whereas in the past we could feel a certain amount of security and stability when it came to our work, our marriage, our environment and our future, now everything seems to be up in the air. The newspapers are full of reports of company mergers where thousands of people are losing their jobs or having to retrain every year. Employers expect flexibility, and if there are no jobs where you live, you will have to move. Some industries have nearly disappeared altogether, and other professions leave highly-trained staff sitting idle because their services are too expensive. Such is the competition in Germany that some dental technical services send their work to China where it can be carried out more cheaply!

An increasing number of people are now working on a self-employed basis. This is because employers today prefer to subcontract work or to employ freelancers as and when the need arises. This may be an advantage for those who like working for themselves, but many do not and they struggle to make a living without a regular monthly income. We no longer feel we 'belong' to a particular place of work, and we can no longer be sure that we will be doing the same work in five years' time.

And then there is the environment. The food we eat and the water we drink is no longer safe. The additives which give food a longer shelf life and the fertilisers and pesticides which ensure bigger and better crops, now often turn out to be bad news. Hormones, metals and other chemicals in our tap water have detrimental effects on our health, to an extent we are only beginning to understand. Many species of animals and plants are on the verge of extinction. Global warming, once ridiculed by many scientists, has now begun to spin into action in the form of storms and floods. And then there are the daily reports of armed conflicts around the world which, even long distance, have an unsettling effect on us.

It would be easy to think that it is too late and that there is nothing we can do about these crises, but let me assure you, there *are* solutions. Every big change starts with a small one. In order to affect our environment in a positive way, we need to start by sorting out ourselves. As we work on overcoming our own personal problems, we become more relaxed within ourselves. This means that we are working more efficiently and more effectively. We have better ideas, more zest for life and become more interested in our environment because, rather than using up all our energies to combat our inner turmoil, we have the energy to look at what is going on around us. As we sort ourselves out, we also relate better and more peacefully to others. As we communicate more effectively and more calmly, we get more of what we want to make us content. As we are content, others around us start relaxing and feel more comfortable. This, in turn, helps *them* feel better about themselves, so they can become more contented and work more efficiently. And so it goes on.

This process has an amazing ripple effect – if one person becomes more positive, they will positively influence at least another three people. The effect soon mushrooms into stunning numbers of people who relate well, work more efficiently and create a peaceful and productive atmosphere. This has a real impact, not just within our immediate environment but way beyond it. By working through *Positive Living* and improving your own ways of relating to the world around you, you are taking the first step, not just to making your own life better but also that of those around you!

In Part I of this book, we will take a closer look at the pressures and problems that result from our lifestyle changes in present times and learn the principles for overcoming them so we may all live fulfilled lives. In order to be happy in life, we need to have good emotional and physical health, satisfying relationships with relatives and friends, ideally a special person as a life companion, and we need to enjoy the work we are doing, be it at home (with or without children), paid employment or freelance work. And we need to have a purpose in life – something that makes us *want* to get up in the morning and start our day. In Part II, we focus in on specific problems that may be getting in the way of you living fulfilled and contented lives. These are divided up into the areas of Emotional and Physical Health, Relationships, and the Workplace and there are detailed strategies for overcoming problems within each of them.

By using the power of your subconscious mind and the other practical methods contained in this book, you can make your personal dreams and visions come true. I wish you every happiness and success.

PART ONE

.

Positive Living – Challenges for the 21ˢᵗ Century

CHAPTER ONE

New Century – Same Old Problems?

W hen you are leading a busy life, there is seldom time to step back and reflect on how things have changed. For many people, it is only on New Year's Eve that they stop for a moment and think about what has happened over the past year and where they want to go in the new one.

With the recent turn of the century, we have had an opportunity to look back much further in time and marvel at the staggering developments that have taken place since 1900. The progress in health, lifespan, technology and living standards is striking, and the quality of life today, even for people on only modest incomes, is so much better than it was then. We do have it good! On the other hand, the new century brings new challenges and we need to learn to tackle them constructively.

Mounting stress

There is a lot to be said for the latest technological developments. They make our life easier and more comfortable. They give us access to more information than we have ever had before and this is truly wonderful for all those who want to study or simply learn more about a particular area of interest. We can now research easily and quickly because we have access to a vast array of libraries by way of the Internet.

At the same time, technological progress also brings problems with it, the most noticeable of which being the increased stress levels affecting more and more of us to an extent where health problems begin to manifest. Although stress is not a new problem, the increase in pressures on the individual can no longer be overlooked. Even though we have machines and computers, designed to make our life easier and communication faster, these same machines appear to have become our taskmasters. Because we can type and edit a report in less time than ever and send that same report in seconds to the other end of the world, we are now expected to deliver more reports each day than we did just ten years ago when only a few companies had a computer and none had e-mail. Technology can develop at a prodigious rate, but our mental and physical capacity has limits. We can only work so much and we can only adapt so much before our energy is exhausted.

There are lots of things we *have* to do and there are lots of things we *want* to do, but there are still only twenty-four hours in the day and we still have to eat and sleep. Everything is fast: fast food, fast turnaround time, fast decisions. You are expected to press on with your work, to churn out results, stay polite, friendly and co-operative and not complain about your workload. Profit margins are becoming narrower in many industries, so staff levels are reduced and the remaining employees have to work doubly hard to make up for the lack of support.

The general pace of our life has increased. Information technology today is now such that we can all communicate with each other in several different ways, night or day. We can use letters, phones, faxes, e-mail, telephone and TV conferencing to speak to colleagues anywhere in the world. But, just as we can contact others, they can contact us, and this results in a deluge of communication on a daily basis. If you want to be successful in your career, you have to keep pace with the latest technology and developments. You have to update your IT skills continuously, if you want to stand a chance in the job market. As a business owner, you have to offer better, faster, more efficient service, and you have to do so at the right price.

This work-related stress filters down to all other levels. Working parents experience pressures, tight deadlines, difficult work situations; they come home tired, only to be met by children who have their own needs and who exert pressures on the parents which they often don't have the energy to meet. The children have their own TVs and computers in their rooms, but they return from school to an empty house or irritable, uncommunicative parents. No wonder children are more aggressive and depressed today than ever before. But children have their own problems. Not only the usual ones associated with growing up but also those which stem from an increasingly depersonalised school system, where class sizes are too big and the teachers are too overloaded with administrational matters to give children much individual attention.

These mounting stress levels result in higher absenteeism amongst workers, more physical, mental and emotional health problems, putting an ever-increasing burden on the public health system. Companies are losing millions of working hours a year because of stress-related illness and workers now sue their employers if they feel that work-related stress has resulted in serious health problems for them. As a result, some larger companies are beginning to make stress counselling available for employees who find they need such support. Universities also find that there is an increased need for counselling to help students cope with their emotional and relationship problems. Many students have to support themselves financially throughout their time at university and this puts a high demand on their energy and motivation. Time that should be spent studying is spent earning the money to finance their studies.

An increasing number of people now have more than one job in their working life. While once it was usual to stay in a job one's entire working life, or change companies only occasionally, nowadays an increasing number of people have had at least three entirely different jobs by the time they are forty. This means training and re-training on a regular basis. At the same time, we all need to earn money to pay the bills, the mortgage, for the next holiday and, if you have a family, pay for the children's education. No wonder we are stressed!

Luckily, solutions are available and there is a lot we can do to counterbalance this stress. You will find a great number of positive thinking exercises, as well as practical information about foods and supplements, throughout Part II of the book that will help you bring down your stress levels and promote emotional and physical health. In particular, watch out for the leading themes for each chapter of Part II, 'Self-esteem', 'Tension', 'Communication' and 'Flexibility', The key exercises linked to these themes will help you successfully combat stress levels!

The new technological revolution

Look around your home. Look around your office. Count how many items you possess that have to do with entertainment or information technology. Most households today, no matter what the financial situation, will have at least one of the following items:

- personal cassette player
- personal CD player
- clip-on radio with headphones
- normal radio
- stereo system
- television
- satellite dish
- video recorder
- DVD player
- mobile phone

- computer and printer
- play station

And all this is only in your home! If you looked around your office, you would find many more pieces of technical equipment.

If you have a computer at home, you will probably be linked to the Internet and have an e-mail address, as well as a satellite dish or cable for the TV so that you can shop via the Internet or the TV. If you have children, you are likely to have several TV sets, video recorders and Hi-Fi systems in the house. You may love or hate them, but they are here and they are here to stay. If you haven't got them already, one day soon you will have to start buying and using them, either at home or at work.

Technological progress is now moving faster than ever before. When vinyl records were replaced by tapes, it seemed an amazing development. But remember how quickly tapes were replaced by CDs, and now even they start to look old-fashioned as MP3 music becomes available via the computer. Telephones, radios and television sets are all going digital, and your new computer seems to become obsolete as soon as you have bought it – six months later it is replaced by a better, faster and often cheaper model.

The way we communicate, the way we shop, the way we entertain ourselves is becoming increasingly technology dependent. We need fewer implements to communicate than ever before. Writing a letter used to involve paper, a pen, an envelope and the address details recorded on another piece of paper. Now, all we need is a computer holding all the address details on its hard disc. We just type our message and press a button. Within seconds, the person we wanted to talk to receives our message, the photograph we wanted to show them or the important drawing that they needed for their work.

If we want to amuse ourselves, we don't have to step outside our own front door. We press a button on the remote control and watch whatever we want on the TV. Or we turn on our computer, surf the net, play a computer game or go into chat rooms.

Now that shopping can now be done from home there is no more queuing for the multi-storey car park, unhelpful shop assistants and unpleasant surprises that they don't have your size in stock.

Even though on-line shopping still has teething problems, these will eventually be sorted out. It is becoming increasingly clear that this is a way in which we will do our shopping in the future. This is all very exciting, it saves us time (which we have less and less of) and appears at first glance to make our lives so much easier, but it also isolates us.

Cocooning

There are now more single people living in the UK than ever before. Marriages are no longer forever and relationships do not necessarily last. An increasing number of women have become financially independent of their partners and they can *afford* to leave the relationship if they are not happy in it. At the same time, this gives them more leverage when it comes to waiting for the *right* partner rather than just settling for the *next* partner. Being single is more feasible and more affordable today. Being single with a child is also not uncommon any more. This does not mean that men and women are not striving to be in a good relationship; they are, however, less willing to settle for second best, and I see this as a welcome development. However, if you find being single difficult, *Positive Living* can help you improve your situation. Not only will you find positive thinking strategies to help you become more at ease during your time as a single person, but there is also a specific section on how to find a partner!

For both single people and families, the convenience of in-door shopping is equally obvious. If you are a busy professional single who works all hours, you may not have the time or energy to go shopping or go out to the cinema after work. It is often easier to stay in your cosy, safe home and entertain yourself or shop via the computer. For families, computer games and television programmes can act as an electronic nanny. It keeps the children quiet and gives the parents space for themselves. Television and computers are instantly available, and, as opposed to babysitters or au pairs, they don't bring their boyfriends into your house or drink your wine while you are out! They are just there, and all you have to do is press a button.

And it is *safe* to stay in. When it gets dark outside, you don't have to worry about the inconvenience of catching the last bus home after the cinema or being accosted by beggars while you are on an underground platform. You don't have to feel vulnerable because you are not out there where no one will help you if you are being molested by a junkie who needs your money for the next fix or being assaulted by a psychiatric patient who has not taken his medication . . .

It may not be as bad in the UK as it is in the USA, but we are becoming increasingly worried about our safety. More insurance policies, more burglar alarms, more housesitters while you are away. Just in case. After all, the papers are full of reports of violence and drug-related crime, even in rural areas that once were considered safe.

Our homes are becoming high-tech havens, protecting us from the dangers of the outside world while we have everything we need at our fingertips. But how much does this isolate us? Are we cutting ourselves off too much from the world outside? This can easily happen if you have a demanding job, return home tired and generally have little time left after work to 'live'. Even at the gym, you can be staring at a TV screen in front of you while using the walking machine rather than talking to someone . . .

What happens to human contact, especially when you are single? Is your only contact with your friends an e-mail on your PC screen? And what happens to our children? They spend hours in front of the computer and the TV when once they would have gone out to play with friends. Teenagers spend hours on their mobile phones talking to friends who they saw at school only fifteen minutes before. The mobile phone gives them their own little cocoon, away from the parents and siblings. They used to have to use the phone in the hallway where someone could overhear their conversation and eventually shoo them away, but now they can disappear into their bedroom. Before, parents and siblings could get the occasional grunt out of their fourteen-year-old, now teenagers are totally incommunicado after having exhausted themselves on the phone to their friends . . .

And then there are those people who work from home. Thanks to computer link-ups, more and more people are now able to cut out the daily commute to the workplace. Of course, it is wonderful to have this choice, but it can also reduce direct human contact for those who are single. As every communication happens via computer link, single people working from home can spend days without speaking to a soul.

Family fragmentation

While technological advances can result in us isolating ourselves by staying in rather than going out, working from home can also have its advantages. Parents who are given the opportunity by their employers to work from home are able to see their kids during the day. This can be ideal when the children are still little. Many fathers want to be more involved in the upbringing of their children and working from home is an excellent opportunity to bond with your child. This of course changes rapidly once they start running around and shouting as this makes *you* run around and shout which then disrupts your work.

Today, there are many families where both parents work out of financial necessity. This means that the parents come home tired in the evening, with little energy or patience left to cook a proper meal or help with homework. Tea is often something quick and easy or a takeaway in front of the television. And there is not much conversation while the box flickers through soaps and films and adverts.

A similar scenario unfolds in many of the increasing number of single-parent families. In some school years, up to fifty per cent of the children come from single-parent families where the mother or now also increasingly the father has to fulfil the role of both breadwinner and parent. In extended families, the other family members are now less likely to live nearby, and, if they do, they are not necessarily willing to take over the traditional task of looking after the grandchildren. With older people being generally fitter and healthier than, say, fifty years ago, they are busier after retirement than before, travelling, visiting friends and pursuing hobbies. The stress of bringing up children has gone and they do not want a second dose of the same thing for any length of time.

And even those grandparents who would love to look after their grandchildren may not get the chance because their sons and daughters have to be mobile today if they want to pursue their careers. Where the job requires your physical presence, it is often necessary to move house in order to be near work, and this can mean moving away from the grandparents.

Families today are split up by many factors. The marketplace demands flexible employees who are willing to uproot themselves and their families in order to fit in with work requirements. The traditional family is no longer the norm; instead, single people and single-parent families are as common now as the two-parent family used to be in the past.

What are the consequences of this fragmentation? Extended family members often don't know each other and many traditional family tasks become depersonalised or are taken over by hired help. Household and childrearing help has to be bought in – the au pair looks after your children if you have the money, the television or computer does it if you haven't. The au pair leaves after a year and the children have to start all over with a new person. The TV or computer doesn't change but they are machines without feelings, warmth or conversation.

Single people, single parents and children today are lonelier. They are faced with a big void in their lives and each group tries to fill this as best they can with machines, drugs or therapy sessions. And yet, there is a lot you can do to help yourself, and Part II of the book will show you how to go about it.

Dislocation

Over and above the fragmentation of the family, we are also less firmly rooted in our heritage than we used to be. Our communities in towns and cities have become more international, with people from many different cultures and religions living and working together. This brings with it its own problems. Racism is rife today and causes great distress to those who are at the receiving end, whether they are actually attacked themselves or not. Repeatedly reading reports about groups of people being assaulted or harassed will raise your own stress levels, whether you yourself are a member of that particular group or not. Gay people still have to battle with social prejudice as have members of foreign cultures and religions. This undercurrent of intolerance creates a climate of unease, even amongst those who conform to society's notion of 'normality'.

Nobody wants to be an outsider; everyone wants to 'belong'. But where do we belong? With the internationalisation of society, our ethnic and cultural roots become entangled with a myriad of other influences. We may have tears in our eyes when we hear our national anthem being played at the Olympics, but do we have any true feelings of 'belonging'?

There is less community spirit than there was and most of us haven't ever spoken to our neighbours except for an occasional 'hello'. Some of us have never even *seen* our neighbours, though we live in the house or flat next to theirs. A sense of community is the exception today rather than the rule. This is one of the reasons why the 'care in the community' scheme for psychiatric patients was doomed to failure – we don't nurture our communities any more. There is no network of long-established relationships which helps care for those who cannot look after themselves. This is not because we are fundamentally uncaring. The reason lies in the fact that our society has changed – everyone is out there earning money, even teenagers. No one is at home any more. Suburbs are deserted during the working week. You are rushing to work, you are rushing back home, you are rushing to the supermarket, and you don't look left and you don't look right. Too much to do, no time to stop. And no time to lean over the garden fence and talk with your neighbours.

The only time we form a community is when we feel that we need to protect our rights. Provided people are sufficiently incensed by a perceived injustice, they organise themselves and take the initiative. This is the closest we get to community spirit today. But it is very different from an everyday, peaceful sense of belonging to a group of people who live together in a particular area, who know your name and will help you out when you need it. It is this sense of belonging that most of us have lost.

The less you feel you belong to a community or family network, the more vulnerable you feel. Having to deal with modern day stresses and anxieties is bad enough; doing so without an emotionally supportive network to back you up makes it worse. It takes many years of living in the same place to grow roots, but how many of us still live where we were born? *You* may, but everyone else around you has moved away, so that does not help.

We are more mobile because we have to go where the work is. This may be exciting, but it is also stressful. It is a sign of the times that we travel and move a lot – we go on faraway holidays, we move house within our own country, we move abroad with work, then come back, and so we change our environment many times within a life time. This can be immensely stimulating and it gives us a wealth of new experiences, but it can also make us feel dislocated. So, it is important that we feel at home within ourselves because this will give us an inner 'anchor' to take with us wherever we go. Chapter 3, 'Emotional Health', contains advice to help you achieve greater self-reliance and inner stability and you will find this helpful in promoting your sense of well-being.

Emptiness

When we are unfulfilled, we feel empty. When we feel empty, a spontaneous need arises in us to fill that emptiness, however temporary this may be. One way is to use substances which will help us forget this hollow inner feeling. These can be drugs or alcohol for example, and their function is to blot out what we don't want to see or feel. If we resort to this type of solution, we are clearly not solving the underlying problem of emptiness but creating an additional one, namely that of an addiction.

Another way of attempting to fill the inner void is by obsessively changing either your own outer appearance or that of your immediate environment by buying new clothes or amassing possessions. When consumerism becomes a substitute for a lack of meaning in your life rather than being an occasional pleasure, we need to look a bit more closely at our concepts and attitudes.

Some of those whose education is not good enough, who are psychologically vulnerable, socially disadvantaged or who have become outcasts for any other reason, drop out of the rat race and become depressed, violent or aggressive towards themselves, mutilating their health through drugs or alcohol. But, perversely, it is also some of those who *do* achieve who are increasingly becoming involved in these desperate strategies to keep themselves going. If failure endangers well-being and psychological equilibrium, so can success.

The question we need to ask is, what do the unstable successful person and the drop-out have in common? What makes them rely on drugs, drink or other crutches to get through the day? For the successful, it cannot be the workload or the pressures of having a career that pushes them towards breakdown. If those criteria were an automatic precondition for stress, everyone who is successful would be stressed, but this is not always so. For the drop-outs without a job or a home, it cannot just be the lack of education or a difficult childhood. If this were enough to make people drop out of what is considered to be a 'normal' life, there would be millions more drop-outs in the UK. Instead, there are a great number of people who have achieved their goals *despite* a lack of education or *despite* a dreadful childhood. This is very encouraging because it shows that there are solutions out there to help us overcome obstacles that have been put in our way by circumstances. No matter what has happened to us in the past, no matter where we come from, we can actively participate in making our life richer and more fulfilling. This is exactly what you can achieve when you use the positive thinking methods described in Part II of this book. Look out for the sections on loneliness and boredom!

What is it that makes you come through against all the odds and keeps you sane despite the pressure of work? It is the sense that your life has *meaning*, that there is a valid reason why you are here and that purposeful actions on your part are actually worthwhile. Without a sense of meaning, you have nothing: you may as well be dead. With a sense of meaning, you can focus, you are motivated and you develop initiative and a will to see things through. Just look at your child who learns in the shortest possible time how to work a computer, while that same child appears to be unable to grasp the basics of maths. Using the computer has meaning, it promises the rewards of enjoyment, challenge and adventure, and the possibility of being one up on their classmates. A sense of meaning creates energy and positive action, and, ultimately, it creates results. By living purposefully, not only are our lives made more enjoyable, but also less stressful and more fulfilled.

Environmental concern

We are now at a stage where we begin to witness the consequences of our actions over the last century. Technology and medicine have advanced rapidly, and lots of the resulting innovations have been used to make our lives more comfortable, more convenient or safer. But many of these new ways of dealing with our environment are coming back to haunt us.

We are in a position where a number of foods are no longer safe to eat. The increase in allergies which more and more people are suffering from today is attributed to the effects of artificial fertilizers, preservatives and colourings in our foods. Our bodies are simply not equipped to deal with them. The increased demand for organic foods over the last few years shows how seriously people take these health concerns. The water from our taps, although officially declared safe for drinking, has been shown to contain hormones and heavy metals which even intense filtration cannot remove. So even when we try to live healthily and spend a lot of money on organically produced meat, we still ingest artificial hormones from the water we use to cook our food in. Phthalates (plastic softening agents) used in the packaging of foods in supermarkets may ruin our best efforts as they have been shown to act in the same way as oestrogen. If you wrap your food in cling film or other plastic containing phthalates, the artificial oestrogen wanders into your food and, consequently, into your body . . .

And the list goes on. The air we breathe is polluted, and so is the soil we use to grow our vegetables and fruit. Animals are given growth hormones so they yield more meat and antibiotics to allow more intensive farming. More and more of our staple foods are processed, resulting in the loss of most of their goodness.

From our most immediate environment, the detrimental effects extend out further into nature. The emission of exhaust fumes from road and air traffic, together with our past heavy use of CFC gases, has resulted in a hole in the ozone layer, causing significant climate change. Nuclear technology has landed us with huge problems concerning the storage of radioactive waste, as well as the constant threat of nuclear accidents as at Chernobyl.

The good news is that we are now more aware of all these problems and are taking them more seriously than ever before. An increasing number of people take personal action on a regular basis to help the environment. This can be by taking waste paper to a paper bank or separating out glass for recycling, or by joining environmental organisations. Membership rates have been growing massively over the last twenty years.

Our attitude is slowly changing from profit and mindless consumption towards thoughtful and considerate handling of our resources. More needs to be done in the future to limit the damage that has already been inflicted on the environment and people who are courageous and positive will be needed to take on these tasks. A great deal of awareness and a sense of responsibility are necessary from each individual to contribute to this effort. Nothing will be saved, repaired or improved if we all take the attitude that the problems are already out of control and that our individual contribution would be worthless and ineffective. Just now, it is vital that each of us understands that he is a citizen of the world and, as such, is able to make a difference with his positive attitude and actions to help preserve our environment.

Not everyone is cut out to be a leader, but all of us have the ability to contribute to the process of protecting our environment in our own way. Lots of small contributions make one big contribution, so let's stay positive! Only then can we act efficiently and make a difference. *Positive Living* will show you ways of how to develop the necessary constructive attitude to do just that.

International conflict

When the conflict in Kosovo was at its height, I was invited to give talks in bookshops in southern Germany. At the start of every talk, I asked my audience what made them feel afraid at the moment, and one answer kept recurring: the war in Yugoslavia.

We have been fortunate in not having had to live through another World War since the 1940s, but there have been lots of other conflicts in countries around us. In the UK, there have been the Northern Ireland troubles, still simmering now, although a great deal has been achieved recently to bring the bloodshed to an end. Then there was the Gulf War, Afghanistan, Yugoslavia, the ongoing crisis in Iraq, as well as nuclear escalation between India and Pakistan. America and others get involved, imposing sanctions, sending peacekeeping forces or flying punitive missions over offending countries. The wars may be further away from home, but with long-range missiles now in the hands of Third World countries, the world has become a much smaller place when it comes to retaliation.

With extensive media coverage of conflicts all over the world, we are confronted on a daily basis with news of wars and the sabre rattling of foreign dictators threatening revenge for our involvement in their internal or external conflicts. This constant exposure may have hardened us to other countries' miseries and disasters, but global unrest still affects us, if not consciously, then certainly at a subconscious level. Seeing others lose everything, especially when it is close to home, touches on our own insecurities. Also, what happens to others in the world affects us at a deep, communal level and has a substantial influence on our stress levels, particularly when we are already feeling depressed or below par for other reasons.

So what can we do to change how we feel? And is there anything at all we can do to promote peace in this world around us? The amazing answer to both questions is 'yes'.

As far back as the 1970s, scientific studies were carried out in America and Canada about the correlation of positive attitudes and crime rates. The results show that twenty-four cities in which one per cent of the population had been instructed in Transcendental Meditation in 1972 displayed decreased crime rates during the next five years. Similarly, two later studies found a significant reduction in weekly fatalities due to car accidents, homicides and suicides in the United States and Canada in the period between 1983 and 1985 when one per cent of the population engaged in regular positive thought through meditation.

These are very encouraging findings because they prove that positive thought can effect enormous improvements, not just within ourselves but also for the world around us. If increased positivity can lower crime rates, violent fatalities and conflict, then we owe it to ourselves and the society we live in to do all we can to reduce our stress levels and become happier people.

CHAPTER TWO

From Negative To Positive

For many people, resolving a personal problem in their life can become the central point of attention around which everything else revolves. When there is an issue in our lives that seems to defy us, we usually try to cope with it by ourselves to begin with. We read up on the problem to get pointers as to how we could resolve it. We try to understand what is causing it in the first place and hope that through this insight, it will go away. If it doesn't, we eventually seek professional help, hoping that this will put an end to the problem.

Whatever approach we choose, it is important that we pull our weight. If we are dogged by a health problem, it is essential that we monitor our own actions to see if we are doing anything that causes or aggravates it. If we have an emotional issue that makes us unhappy, we need to be prepared to examine what we can do to help ourselves leave the past behind. There comes a point when we need to stop blaming our parents and/or our partner and take positive action to create the circumstances which will make us happier.

Positive Living shows you ways out of a number of emotional and physical fixes. With the help of some simple techniques you can do a great deal to help yourself overcome your limitations. All that is required is that you make the application of these methods your purpose for the next few weeks. You can achieve a lot by yourself. No doctor, no therapist, just you and your mind!

Positive living through positive thinking

Those of you who have already read *Positive Thinking* will be familiar with the principles of positive thinking. I will go over the basics here for those readers who don't know them yet or who want to refresh their memory. Also, I have added some new aspects to the approach to help you adopt a more constructive frame of mind so you can live more positively.

The main points of my particular way of using positive thinking are as follows. To lead a happy and fulfilled life, you need to:

- take responsibility for your own well-being
- strive for the best possible relationships (partner, friends) in your life
- leave detrimental relationships
- strive to be truly yourself
- look after your health
- use your mind to its full potential
- understand what makes you tick
- have time for yourself
- do things that give meaning to your life

In other words, in order to be happy you need to create the environment where you can fulfil your true potential. If you are doing it my way, there is very little room for blaming others, even though others may be to blame for your unhappiness in the first place. Life is *not* fair and, whether you believe in reincarnation or not, you need to get on with what you have in your life *right now*. Every minute you spend blaming others is a minute you could have spent thinking about how you can change your situation for the better. Some people you have around you may be bad for you and you will have to leave them behind because they stop you from being yourself or from being happy. Others may have done you damage financially or physically. If you feel it appropriate and important, then use every legal means to call them to account. After that, you must move on, otherwise you are inflicting damage on yourself. If someone has damaged you psychologically, go to a good therapist to sort out your feelings about the past, and then move on. It is the moving on which this book is all about.

Helping the body help itself

Our bodies are true miracles of life force. When you begin to consider how many processes are happening in the body each single minute of our lives, it quickly becomes clear that no man-made machine, however sophisticated, could ever begin to match the complexity of the human body. While you are sitting reading this page, your heart keeps beating, your diaphragm keeps moving with your lungs, supplying oxygen to your system and brain, your digestion is working away if you have eaten recently, blood is pumping around the body, your temperature is being adjusted and readjusted, and a hundred thousand other things are happening which you are not even aware of. And all this continues to work, even though we might not be looking after our bodies very well! We don't exercise enough to help our lymph system do its work, we eat too much and often all the wrong things, we do not drink enough water and are often dehydrated, and still our bodies function. It is amazing what we can get away with. We overwork, abuse our body with stimulants, don't get enough rest and allow the stress to build up by not taking enough breaks and then we wonder why we suffer from sleeplessness, irritation, depression and all sorts of other physical and emotional warning signs.

The body is a finely-tuned machine which has the ability to right itself when it is out of balance. What the body needs from us by way of maintenance is the following:

- good, nutritious food
- plenty of water
- air
- light
- moderate exercise

If we provide our body with these fundamentals it can function well and stands a much better chance of rebalancing itself in times of stress.

Things that are detrimental to the body's smooth functioning are:

- eating sugars (natural and artificial) in foods and drinks
- eating too many foods that produce acid in the body (meats) and not enough alkaline foods (vegetables)
- eating too much processed foods
- eating too much
- stressing the body with stimulants (tea, coffee, cigarettes, alcohol, recreational drugs)
- not drinking enough water
- not taking enough fresh air
- not spending enough time outside in the daylight
- not taking enough exercise

It is not always necessary to eat all the right foods. No one can do that. But it is certainly necessary to strive to eat most of the right foods as often as possible. And water cannot be replaced by any other drink. Lemonades and soft drinks all contain sugars of some description, juices are treated like food by the stomach and even herbal teas, unless they are very weak, need to be processed by your body. Water, on the other hand, provided it is still water and not too cold, can enter directly into your system, where it helps the nerves and all the organs to function better.

Providing your body with oxygen

We breathe all the time, night and day, while we are awake or asleep. Breathing happens by itself and we don't pay much attention to it unless it becomes unusually rapid. This may happen when we get upset, when we have been running or when we experience fear or panic attacks. Unless we can recognise a logical reason for our accelerated breath, we tend to become scared. Breathing is a fundamental body function and, if this function is impaired, for example if we suffer from asthma, our life is potentially in danger.

On a subtler level, our breathing pattern is shaped by our personality type and by our past experiences. If you spend long stretches of time being nervous or scared, you will automatically hold your breath a lot, even when the original stress is no longer there. The body learns a certain tension pattern during stressful times and then hangs on to that pattern 'just in case'. However, if you don't breathe regularly enough, not enough oxygen gets to the brain and this means you cannot think optimally. This, in turn, results in you making mistakes more easily, thus making you feel more anxious . . . A vicious circle.

It is therefore worth your while paying a bit of attention to your breathing.

Breathing Exercise

- Close your eyes and *listen* to your breathing.

- Feel the *upward* movements of your body as you breath in and the *downward* movement as you exhale.

- Put one hand on your belly above your navel. Make sure this area is rising with every *in-breath* and deflating with every *out-breath*. This way, you breathe correctly.

Check briefly a couple of times during the day that your breathing is correct. Even if your breathing pattern has been incorrect over many years, you can 'retrain' yourself to make it better.

'Slow foods' – keeping body and mind together

The fast pace of life we live today seems to require food that can be prepared and eaten quickly. The quickest way is eating straight out of the packet (crisps, biscuits, chocolate) or sticking a packet into the oven or microwave (ready-cooked meals, processed food). It is a fact that most of us eat processed food, at least occasionally. I do. Some of us eat it all the time; in fact processed food, containing sugars and fats, makes up the staple diet of teenagers today.

Ideally, you should not eat junk food at all, but it is not really the junk food that is the problem. A healthy body can deal with a certain amount of inappropriate foods as long as it is given good food in large amounts – natural food that is unprocessed such as fruit and vegetables – and this is where most people's diets fall down.

Especially if you are not one hundred per cent healthy, you *cannot afford* to eat only processed foods. If your body is out of balance through illness, an operation, allergy or psychological trauma, you need more natural foods. They are easily digestible and are readily turned into energy. Processed foods, especially those containing sugars and fats, clog up your system and make it function less well, slowing down or preventing altogether the healing processes. Eating just processed food will eventually lead to illness. If you are not well, physically or psychologically, eating 'slow' foods such as fruit and vegetables gives the body a chance to re-balance itself.

There is no *single* way of eating and drinking that will be perfect for everyone. For some people it is appropriate to be vegetarian; for others it will be detrimental to their health if they cut out meat altogether. Some people can drink ten cups of coffee a day and sleep like a baby at night whereas someone like me cannot even drink one cup without sitting upright in bed for the next three nights in a row . . .

One of the tricks to stay healthy is to listen to your body. It normally gives you lots of warning signals before it becomes unwell, but we don't often have the time or patience to listen. This is why it is useful to eat and concentrate on eating *only*, rather than watch TV at the same time. By focussing on what you are eating, not only do you digest the food better, but you will also notice when you have had enough to eat – a really good slimming aid! Here are some rules of thumb to help you if you want to eat for mental and physical energy:

- Eat more slow foods. Slow foods are the opposite of fast foods. They come from foods that are as close as possible to their original growing state, with as little artificial interference as possible. Slow foods are fruit and vegetables, nuts and seeds.
- Eat more foods that are free from additives.

- Eat more organic foods if you can afford it. Even though organic food is not totally free from pollution, it is still better than foods that have been treated with pesticides, artificial fertilisers and other chemicals.
- Drink more water. Have the best quality water you can get. Make it bottled or filtered water and drink those famous eight large glasses a day. If you drink coffee and tea, you should have one glass of water with every coffee or tea you have. This is in addition to the eight large glasses of water! The reason for the extra water is that tea and coffee dehydrate the body.
- If you must eat junk food, enjoy it. There is no point in going on a guilt trip because you have just had a Coke or a fried breakfast. Concentrate on it, enjoy it and then think what you can next feed your body that will be good for it. In the battle of taste buds versus health, don't put yourself under stress by reproaching yourself for the unhealthy things you eat or drink. Stress will only make you want to eat more of the wrong foods. As long as you balance out the unhealthy foods with lots of slow foods, you will be OK.
- Eat a greater variety of foods. Once you discover which foods you like, you tend to eat the same things time and again. If you only eat and drink a small variety of foods and they become your staple diet, you can develop an allergy to them. It is healthier to have a variety of different foods, eaten in rotation during the week. For example, you could have cereal one morning, some toast and jam the next, some fruit the next morning and so on. Don't diet on particular foods only for any length of time. Instead, establish good eating habits that you can keep up for the rest of your life.

The power station of the subconscious

The things we believe about ourselves and the world around us will always manifest in our reality. If we are convinced, for whatever reason, that we are unimportant, we will not only live our lives as if we were unimportant, but we will also expect others to treat us without respect. Maybe we were not given positive attention as children, or maybe we are living with a partner who does not respect our wishes or feelings. No matter how long ago a belief was formed, it can stay with you until the end of your days if you don't work on changing that belief.

Anything we learn or experience in life is stored in our subconscious mind. If I believe that I am unworthy, I will see the world through the belief filter that says 'I am unworthy'. So if someone keeps me waiting, I 'know' why that is – because I'm unworthy. The possibility that my business partner got held up because the train was delayed does not even enter my mind. If someone compliments me on a piece of work I have done, I don't believe him. Because I 'know' I'm unworthy, the other person is either too stupid to see it or they are being dishonest in praising my work. In other words, everything I experience in my life will be assessed through my belief filter. If the incoming information fits with my belief, it confirms it even more, if it contradicts my belief, I simply won't accept the experience as true. So, if your belief is a negative one, you will never give yourself a chance of balancing the negativity through positive experiences. Your subconscious negative belief will not allow you to do so.

It is our subconscious mind that houses all our memories, beliefs, emotions and automatic physical responses. It is our subconscious mind that runs our life and determines how happy and successful we are. Even though we don't normally try and influence the subconscious levels of our minds, it is actually quite easy to do. Here are some simple techniques to help you take control:

AFFIRMATIONS

Affirmations are short, positive sentences that give us a lift. They need to be positively phrased and ideally they should be constructed in the present tense.

Examples

Problem: Overeating
Affirmation: 'My appetite is becoming smaller and smaller' or 'I am satisfied with less and less food'.

Problem: Smoking
Affirmation: 'I can let go of what is superfluous in my life.' or 'I can learn to stay calm and relaxed as I become a happy non-smoker.'

Affirmations should be used frequently throughout the day, at least three times a day ten times in a row. You can use them as:

- thoughts
- words spoken out loud
- words you write down

It doesn't particularly matter *how* you repeat your affirmation; the main thing is that you do so frequently and consistently over a period of two to three weeks. It also does not matter whether you sit down, lie down or stand up while you are saying or thinking them, whether your eyes are open or closed. However, what does help is if you say or think them *with feeling*, as if you believed them.

There are two things that happen when you say your affirmation. Firstly, a new message is imprinted in your subconscious mind. Through repetition of the same positive message, a memory groove is established in your subconscious mind. This eventually becomes a new belief that will help you achieve your chosen aim. Secondly, as you think the affirmations, not only do you send them inwards into your own mind but you also send them outside yourself into the world beyond where they help attract favourable circumstances that will help you achieve your aim. For instance, you may find you bump into someone who points you in the right direction for the new job you were seeking, or you meet someone who invites you to a party where you meet your ideal partner.

Tips and tricks
1. If you construct your own affirmations, make sure they are *positively phrased*. 'I lose my fear of spiders' may sound OK, but you are keeping the link between 'fear' and 'spiders' going. What you really want is to stay calm and relaxed when a spider is near you, so a much more effective affirmation could be 'I can learn to stay calm and relaxed in the presence of spiders.'

2. Make sure your affirmation is phrased in the present tense. Avoid words like 'will', 'would', 'shall' or 'should'. You want to imprint a positive experience into your subconscious mind *now*, not tomorrow or next week.

Example
Not effective: 'Soon I *will* be calm and relaxed with spiders.'

This affirmation pushes the experience of calmness into the future. With every day you use this affirmation, the experience gets pushed further away into the future.

Effective: 'I can be calm and comfortable in the presence of spiders.'

In this example, you are beginning to build a positive belief in your ability to achieve your goal straight away.

Scripts

Scripts are the 'booster package' of positive thinking. They contain an array of positive messages, geared towards supporting you in achieving your aim. In a way, a script is a collection of affirmations linked by a story that describes your progress to your aim.

Example – Overweight

Script: 'With every day, my appetite is getting smaller and smaller. I am eating less than I used to eat in the past. It is as if my stomach had shrunk and can only accept small portions. As I eat less food, I begin to enjoy it more. I chew properly, so that all the taste buds in my mouth are satisfied, completely satisfied. I can even leave something on my plate and that is fine. With every day, the excess weight comes off, slowly and surely.'

The subconscious mind loves pictures. So, as you show it pictures of a smaller stomach, happy taste buds and a slimmer figure, it 'gets the message' even more clearly than with affirmations alone. The memory groove in the subconscious helps establish a positive belief even more firmly. As you believe your appetite is smaller, it actually becomes smaller and this, in turn, helps you lose the excess pounds.

The best ways of using scripts is either to record them on a cassette and listen to them on your personal stereo, or to copy them on to a separate piece of paper which you carry around with you and read several times a day.

Scenarios

In a scenario you imagine that you have already achieved your aim. You see yourself being the person you really want to be, confident, slim, a non-smoker or whatever else you set as your goal. If you are ill, you see your body being repaired from the inside and your health restored. For scenarios, it is best to close your eyes.

Example – Overweight

Scenario: With your eyes closed, imagine yourself having lost all your excess weight, imagine standing in front of a mirror in a smaller size outfit which fits you perfectly. See the result in your mind's eye, feel the happy or elated feelings that come with having achieved your aim, imagine running your hands along your slimmer contours.

Involve as many senses as possible when you imagine your scenario. The more your visualisation is supported by all the senses (sight, sound, touch, taste, smell) the larger the quantity of positive information that is downloaded into your subconscious mind.

Throughout this book you will find suggestions for affirmations, scripts and scenarios, tailor-made for particular problem areas. This does not mean that you cannot construct your own. If you don't like a particular script, write your own. Just make sure you follow the basic rules as outlined in the 'Affirmations' section (*see* pages 34–35).

Tips and tricks

1. A good way of finding out whether an affirmation, a script or scenario hits the spot for you (and consequently will be effective) is by doing the following:

- Sit down and with your eyes closed place your hand on your navel.
- Now think your affirmation, script or scenario as intently as possible. If you get a good, 'happy' feeling in the area underneath your hand, your affirmation, script or scenario is good. If the feeling under your hand is neutral or uncomfortable, you need to change your affirmation, script or scenario until it feels physically 'happy' when you think about it.

Using this book

You have probably bought this book because you were looking for the solution to a personal problem that is holding you back at the moment. You can now look in the index at the end of the book for references to your particular problem and, if you are already familiar with positive thinking methods, check whether the suggested affirmations, scripts and scenarios are suitable for you. If they are not, revamp them in a way that makes them work for you.

Each section in Part II has an introduction in which the causes and effects of the particular problem are discussed. I would urge you to read this. To know what has caused your problem may not solve it for you, but it gives you a much better lever on how to tackle an issue if you understand how it came about. This is a quick way of using the book if you have little time and want to get started immediately.

You will find that each of the four chapters in Part II – Emotional Health, Physical Health, Relationships and Work Life – has a leading theme. This theme will help you to obtain a positive foundation for the rest of the chapter and it is the pivotal point around which all the other issues and problems in that chapter are grouped. For example, in Chapter 5 'Relationships', our theme is 'communication', since being able to talk openly and constructively is one of the major, if not *the* major, precondition under which a relationship can develop and thrive. In the 'Work Life' chapter, the theme is 'flexibility', as this is the skill you will need in today's ever changing work environment to keep on top of things and make your work enjoyable and rewarding.

So, before you launch into your particular problem area, spend some time working through the section's theme first by using the affirmations, scripts and scenarios to give yourself a solid foundation for any other work you may then want to do on yourself. This will help you gain a deeper understanding and help you become more skilled in tackling any issues that you would like to work through in your life.

PART II

.

Solutions
for Positive
Living

CHAPTER THREE

Emotional Health

In the last few decades we have come to understand how important emotional health is to our overall well-being. It is estimated that nowadays seventy per cent of all physical illnesses are psychosomatic by nature, meaning that those illnesses are created or exacerbated by psychological factors. From my professional experience, I would say the true figure is much higher, with anxiety and depression the most common emotional problems that can go on to cause physical complaints.

There are many reasons why more people today complain about emotional problems. For one thing, we are clearly more stressed. There are numerous studies that indicate that work-related stress and the illnesses it causes are on the increase – the CBI reported that absence from work cost businesses £10 billion in 1999. But we are also more aware of psychological problems. With more information available and greater media coverage of mental and emotional problems, we are now better able to give a complaint its appropriate name. Whereas, a few decades ago, it would have been considered self-indulgent to talk about anxiety, this problem is now taken much more seriously, not just by the sufferer, but also by the medical profession. Rather than eliciting the comment 'Just pull yourself together!' friends and family may now suggest that the sufferer seek professional help.

Body and mind are constantly in close and immediate communication with one another. If something is traumatic for the mind, it will go on to have repercussions on the physical level. Equally, if events stress the body, such as operations, accidents or lack of nutrients, there will be consequences for the mind. If you are in permanent discomfort physically, to whatever degree, this will wear you down emotionally. A simple example is a headache. When your head hurts, your concentration is less good and you are more likely to make mistakes. In turn, this will annoy and frustrate you – an emotional response even more detrimental to your concentration. Equally, if a particular life situation stresses you, such as a difficult customer you have to deal with at work, you become emotionally overwrought and this can create a physical symptom, namely a headache.

Even though there are these close links between emotional and physical health, I have dealt with them in two separate chapters to make it easier for you to find the problem area that is relevant to you. In doing so, I have allocated the various topics to either the physical or emotional chapter according to where they are generally thought to belong. But please bear in mind that there are lots of crossovers between the 'Physical Health' and 'Emotional Health' chapters.

SELF-ESTEEM

Time and time again, in my practical work with clients, I find that low self-esteem is the root cause of emotional problems, and this is why I would like to make this the leading theme for this chapter. Solid self-esteem is vital to your emotional well-being, and once your self-esteem is up and running, many other problems will fall by the wayside. Think about it. If you value yourself, you will treat your own needs as important, so if something is wrong in your life, you will sort it out because you feel you are worth it. When your boss wants to give you more work than you can handle, you will point this out or simply refuse to accept the extra workload. When you value yourself, you don't take problems lying down. You respect yourself and you respect others. You think well of yourself. You can feel happy and pleased about your achievements while, at the same time, calmly working on those areas of your personality that need improving.

In order to find out how solid your self-esteem is, check your answers to the following questions:

- What do you think of yourself when you are alone and no one is looking?
- Are you pleased with who you are?
- Are you on your own side or one of your own worst enemies?
- When you look at what you have done with your life so far, does it fill you with happiness or despair?

A lot of our happiness depends on how well we get on with ourselves, how much we are in tune with our needs and how skilfully we utilise our inner resources. The most crucial question, however, is whether you consider yourself to be *as worthy as everyone else*. If the answer is 'no', you are likely to encounter problems both in your work and in your private life because either you hide your light under a bushel or you react in an overly aggressive way to others.

There can be many reasons why we don't like ourselves. While it is true that some of us are born more confident than others, low self-esteem is usually something we learn early on in life from people who don't like themselves. People who are genuinely happy and contented have no need to put down, ridicule or constantly criticise others. So take a moment and ask yourself, '*Where have I learnt to believe that I am worth less than others?*' Was it from a parent, another relative, a teacher or, later in life, a partner? With hindsight, try to assess how reliable their assessment of you was. How 'together', how successful, how happy was this person? What do you think of them now you are grown up yourself?

But it is not only other people who can damage the view we hold of ourselves. Sometimes, we are caught up in a situation where we feel we have failed and then we blame ourselves for not having done better as is shown in Harry's story (page 47).

Affirmations
- I am as worthy as everyone around me, no matter what happened in the past.
- My confidence and self-esteem are building steadily and solidly every day in a positive way.
- I gradually develop greater inner harmony and my calm approach allows me to feel more confident.

Script
I am turning over a new leaf right now. I have decided that, with immediate effect, I am just as important and worthwhile as everyone else. No matter what happened in the past, I am now starting again. No matter how I have been treated in the past, I am now making a fresh start. I now make my own rules and I live and act according to these rules. My rule says '*I am worthwhile*' and I am treating myself accordingly. I switch to positive and speak to myself in a friendly and respectful manner. I am enjoying the positive feelings that well up in me as I speak to myself lovingly. I am making a new start and enjoy the pleasant changes which come with my new strength and decisiveness. My self-worth is beginning to develop in constructive and enjoyable ways.

Scenario
Imagine that you have a little guardian angel sitting on your shoulder, giving you moral support by pointing out your good points to you.

Please work through this self-esteem section first before going on to tackle any of the other emotional issues that might be a problem in your life at the moment. Self-esteem can be built up with positive thinking, as is shown in the following case history of one of my clients.

Harry's Story

Harry (27) came to see me because he found it difficult to converse with others in a social setting. He was a big, solidly built man who appeared to be physically strong, but when he sat in the pub he felt most uncomfortable when it came to speaking to others. In his therapy sessions, it turned out that when he was eighteen his parents had both gone abroad to work, taking Harry's younger brother with them. Harry was left behind to look after his sixteen-year-old sister Samantha. Harry had just lost his job and was therefore at home, so the parents decided that he could look after Samantha who was still at school.

Harry had a nightmare time for two years until the parents returned. Samantha had been out of control when her parents were still at home, and she became even worse once they had gone away. Harry was unable to prevent her from cutting classes at school. She had friends around the house day and night who would use the house as their own and broke lots of things. When the parents returned, they held Harry responsible for all the damage and reproached him for not having kept better control of his sister. This experience had badly knocked Harry's confidence and self-esteem, and he blamed himself for his 'failure'.

It took quite a few sessions until Harry could let go of this guilt. He began to see that Samantha had already been unruly while the parents were at home. He should never have been given the task of looking after her in the first place. If both his parents could barely control her, how could Harry be expected to do so on his own? Once he accepted that he had been given an impossible task by his parents, he started to relax about this past event and was able to build up his self-esteem. He also started finding it a lot easier to speak to other people in social situations.

EMOTIONAL PROBLEMS AND SOLUTIONS

ANXIETY

Anxiety, in this context, is used as an umbrella term to encompass a number of fear problems. In order of severity, these are:

- apprehension
- worrying
- nerves and fears
- phobias
- panic attacks
- free floating anxiety

Fear can be caused or exacerbated by any number of things:

- physical and mental exhaustion
- prolonged periods of stress
- PMS
- menopause
- psychological trauma (present and past)
- repressed anger
- withdrawal from tranquillisers
- illness
- allergies
- stimulants (tea, coffee, cigarettes)

Apprehension is a slight feeling of alertness where you are aware that a situation could potentially become difficult or unpleasant. If apprehension is felt on a physical level, the feeling is only very slight. It is a state of mental attention where you are closely observing how a given situation is developing. Once the situation is dealt with, apprehension immediately subsides.

WORRYING

Worrying is a state of permanent apprehension. If you are a worrier, you do not have to be in the actual situation itself to worry. Just the *thought* of that situation can evoke feelings of worry. Whereas you would only feel apprehensive about something that is about to happen or will happen very shortly, worrying can be done 'forwards' and 'backwards'. This means that you worry about a future event, then you worry while the event is taking place, and then you continue to worry afterwards about what you should have said or done, whether you offended anyone, made a fool of yourself and so on. Worrying is a much more drawn out affair than feeling apprehensive.

Affirmations

- Things are meant to go well.
- I feel happy and comfortable as I am beginning to believe that things are working out all right.
- I allow myself to release all worry thoughts peacefully and fill my mind with happy anticipation.

Script

I am now beginning to make some subtle changes in my life. I am becoming more active in a very constructive way. Where there is something wrong, I right it if I can. Where there is something to be said, I say it if I can. Where there is something to be done, I do it if I can. And then I relax and enjoy the fact that I have done the best I can. I dwell on my achievements in a loving and positive way. My confidence grows with every day and I am beginning to expect things to go right. It happens more and more often that I forget to worry. It simply slips my mind, and hard as I might try, I simply cannot remember what the negative thought was all about. In the end, I simply adjust my emotions to the fact that I now have to feel happy and optimistic.

Scenario

Imagine doing a spring clean in your head. Throw out anything you don't need any more. Imagine all your worry thoughts as rusty old nails that have been stabbing and hurting your mind. Sweep them out of your head and look at all the tools you have at your disposal: courage, determination, understanding, the ability to act and the will to happiness. Remember to use these tools every day in everything you do.

Tips and tricks

1. Be aware that worrying doesn't change anything and is therefore a superfluous activity. If an accident is going to happen, it will do so, whether you worry or not. If you are going to lose your job because your employer is going bankrupt, it will happen, whether you worry or not. Worrying is superfluous. Acting on warning signals, however, is essential! If you feel someone has been drinking too much, don't accept a lift in their car. This is more likely to prevent an accident than you worrying about a potential accident while you are in their car.

2. Some people consider worrying to be a sign of caring. 'I love my children, therefore I have to worry about them constantly'. Worrying has nothing to do with love or caring, it is a sign of insecurity. Work on your self-esteem (*see* pages 44–6) and reduce the level of tension in your body by doing the Relaxation Script (*see* page 90) to help yourself become calmer and more confident.

3. Whenever you catch yourself going into worry thoughts, think 'Cancel!' and think one of your affirmations twenty times in a row. This will help disrupt the automatic worry-loop.

Vanessa's Story

Vanessa knew that her company was about to make her and a number of colleagues redundant. After the initial shock, she began to fret over her situation. She was so convinced that it was impossible for her to find a new job that she did not even apply for suitable positions that were advertised in the papers. Her worries had virtually immobilised her. Like a rabbit in front of the headlights of an oncoming car, Vanessa felt unable to take the appropriate action to secure a new job. Instead, she spent a lot of time feeling resentful towards the company that was making her redundant. At the same time, she was also hoping that they would keep her on after all. But in the end, she had to leave and was now stuck without a job and a redundancy package that would last her only two months. In spite of all this, she could still not mobilise herself into positive action. All she could do was worry.

During a workshop, Vanessa began to understand that she had a number of useful inner resources that she had to start using. Amongst other things, she found that in the past she had been able to use her ability to persist to get things done both at home and at work. Once she became aware of this tool, she found it easier to think about applying for jobs and going for interviews. Even if she did not get a job straight away, she knew she had the ability to keep on looking, so that she would eventually be successful. She later found a new job which was more interesting *and* better paid than the previous one.

PHOBIAS

If you suffer from a fear or 'nerves', then your physical symptoms to a fear stimulus will be stronger than when you just worry. People who get nervous in a particular situation are often also worriers. Their nerves are directed towards at least one specific situation that unsettles them to the point that physical reactions can be observed.

Someone who suffers from exam nerves will worry about an upcoming test for a considerable time before the actual event, and when they enter the exam room, they will feel jittery, have a dry mouth, a lump in their throat and feel cold and sweaty. Some people in this situation can still function and sometimes relax once they realise that they know the answers, but others become virtually immobilised by their fear and they fail the exam. Your ability to do well in exams is diminished when you are nervous. You do not breathe regularly and sometimes you even hold your breath. This prevents enough oxygen getting to the brain resulting in impaired concentration and blocked recall of what you have revised. This is when you 'draw a blank' during the exam, even though you know your stuff. Annoyingly, when someone asks you that same exam question later, you know the answer. It was always there but your fear blocked your access to the answer.

When a fear has got severely out of hand, we speak of a phobia. Here, the fear of a particular situation or object is so strong that you have to avoid it altogether. Even though you know that your phobia is irrational, you still cannot free yourself from your fear. A phobia can be attached to a social situation, such as eating in public or using public lavatories. Other phobias occur in conjunction with certain events, for example thunderstorms, fireworks or popping balloons, and yet other phobias relate to specific objects or animals. Some people are petrified of birds, cats or moths, while others cannot bear to wear any clothes with buttons. A phobia usually requires professional help as it can severely disrupt the sufferer's life. This is especially true of agoraphobia, where people are afraid to leave the house or to be left in the house by themselves. Some agoraphobics are so terrorised by their fear that they have not left the house in years.

A phobia is different from an ordinary fear, and there are three components that distinguish it:

- The fear is *persistent* over a long period of time.
- The fear is *unreasonable*, but even though you can see this, the recognition does not help you get rid of the phobia.
- Having a phobia always entails you *avoiding* the feared object, situation or activity.

For our affirmations, script and scenario, I will use a phobia of birds as an example. If you suffer from a different phobia, you will need to adapt the following suggestions to fit your particular case. This is easy to do: just read through the rules governing affirmations and scripts (*see* pages 34–6) to refresh your memory and then change the following suggestions to match your particular fear.

Affirmations

- I can learn to be calm and relaxed when I encounter birds.
- I am getting stronger and stronger every day and enjoy sharing the world with all kinds of animals, including birds.
- Gently and calmly I ease myself into the enjoyable presence of birds.

Script

I know that my subconscious mind is working for me day and night to shift thoughts and ideas to the right place in my mind. Things that used to upset me in the past now just calm and relax me. To my surprise and my delight I am noticing how I am getting calmer and more comfortable as I am walking around outside. I am moving with confidence; I feel in control. I calmly walk wherever I want to go to. I am unphased by any animals that might cross my path. Birds can walk by my side, in front of me or behind me. I feel calm and relaxed. Birds can sit on roofs and on trees. I feel calm and relaxed. Birds can fly off roofs and they can fly off trees. I feel calm and relaxed. Birds can fly above me or next to me. I feel calm and relaxed. And as my subconscious mind hears me thinking these thoughts, it puts the most comfortable and beneficial feelings into action for me. I am beginning to feel more and more relaxed at the thought of birds, at the presence of birds. It delights and surprises me how comfortable I can be as I think of birds, as I see birds, as I watch them fly, above me, next to me. I am calm and relaxed, I feel free and easy and move effortlessly through a world that contains birds.

Scenario

Imagine yourself in the presence of an animal that you like, for example a cat. Imagine how pleasant it is to be with this cat. Imagine being with the cat so that you can feel those pleasant feelings while you are thinking about the cat. While you stay in your thoughts with the cat and the pleasant feelings, imagine a bird walking past you, first far away from you, then closer to you.

Tips and tricks

1. If you find the scenario too difficult to do, make sure you relax first of all. Use the Breathing Exercise (*see* page 30) and the Relaxation Script (*see* page 90) to start with, then begin to imagine the phobia scenario.

2. If this is still too difficult to do, then imagine the following:

a)   Close your eyes and watch on the screen in your mind how *another person* strokes a cat and has a bird walk past them at a considerable distance. See the other person remain calm and happy. Once you can watch this scene calmly on the screen, continue to b).

b)   Keep your eyes closed and continue to stay outside the screen. Watch *yourself* in the screen calmly stroking a cat while a bird walks across the screen at a great distance from you. Run this film past you until you can watch it calmly. Once you have achieved this, go on to the next step.

c)   Keep your eyes closed and rewind the film on the screen. Now step into the screen and be in the film. Feel yourself calmly stroking the cat and enjoying it. Feel your inner calmness as you watch a bird walk past you at a great distance. As you are getting more comfortable with this image, re-run the film and have the bird walk by closer to you.

PANIC ATTACKS

Panic attacks are a particular kind of phobia. Panic attacks initially happen very suddenly, usually at a time when the sufferer has been under emotional stress for a while. Depending on where the first panic attack happens, the person will subconsciously link the panic attack with that particular location. Say for example you are very upset about a relationship problem while you are on a plane. If as a consequence of this emotional overload you produced your first panic attack at this moment, you would associate flying with panic feelings and therefore try and avoid flying. What you are really avoiding are the panic attacks.

A panic attack is a very unsettling event. You feel terrorised and extremely frightened, and these feelings are accompanied by a variety of physical symptoms. Some people are rushed into hospital with a suspected heart attack when what they are having is a panic attack. In reality, there is nothing wrong with their body at all. Their heart is healthy and working perfectly well; it is only the very strong fear that rouses the body's responses to a level where there is so much adrenalin released into your system that it makes the heart race and all the other 'fight or flight' responses kick into action.

Signs of a panic attack are:

- racing heart
- cold sweat
- inability to move
- numbness
- trembling
- feeling faint
- feeling compelled to leave the panic-inducing situation immediately

Affirmations
- Panic attacks are a nuisance but harmless. I am perfectly sane and healthy.

- I am slowly becoming calmer and more in control as I am dealing with people around me and sorting out my life.
- I can be afraid and still breathe. I am safe and secure.

Script

I am running on emotional overload. This is fine; it happens to everyone at some time in their life. I am just ordinary in that way. I am now sorting out whatever needs to be tackled in my life to help myself reduce my emotional stress levels. I am strong and deal with problems in a positive and constructive way. I am determined to improve my circumstances. I am confident and strong. Slowly, I am noticing how I am getting calmer and calmer, feeling more in control. My breathing is even and regular, and my comfortable breathing relaxes me. As I am breathing deeply and comfortably in, and as I am breathing all the way out, my head is clear and I can think succinctly and calmly about everyday matters. Even when I get stressed, I can still breathe. As I concentrate on my breathing, I relax. With every breath I take in, I breathe in what I need. With every breath I expel, I breathe out what I no longer want. I am safe and I am secure. Nothing can touch me.

Scenario

Use a similar scenario as described for phobia. See yourself in the situation that normally gives rise to panic attacks and imagine yourself dealing with it easily and effortlessly. If this is still a problem, use the strategies for phobias, (*see* 'Tips and tricks' 2, page 54).

Tips and tricks

1. Use the above script in the evenings before going to bed.

2. During the day, use the following script:

'Today is my big day! I am determined to produce the most amazing panic attack that anyone has ever seen. I am determined to make a spectacle of myself and get as much attention as I can. I will throw myself to the floor and scream and shout. I am going to do everything I can to foam at the mouth so that people around me are shocked and taken aback by my performance. No more half measures! I am determined to produce a really big one today, and tomorrow it will be in all the papers!'

Write out this script on to a separate little piece of paper and carry it with you wherever you go. Read the note twenty times in a row, three times a day, when you are *not* panicky or *before* you go into a situation that normally makes you panic.

DO NOT CHANGE THE WORDING OF THE SCRIPT! It is very important that you make out that you are going to produce the panic attack *on purpose*, so copy the script exactly as you find it on this page.

This technique is very powerful and works extremely well. It is based on the fact that when you are trying to produce a spontaneous effect on purpose, you can't do it. (Try and hiccup on purpose. You will find that it is not possible!) I sometimes invite my clients to have a panic attack for me there and then, right here in my consulting room, and every single time I find that they are incapable of producing it on demand!

3. Practise proper breathing. Make sure you *breathe in* with your stomach coming *out*, and *breathe out* with your stomach deflating. If you suffer from panic attacks, the most important thing to do is to *breathe out fully*, so squeeze your tummy muscles back when you are practising breathing out. Practise proper breathing several times a day. An ideal opportunity is when you have to wait at traffic lights or in a queue at the supermarket.

Claudia's Story

A friend of mine, Claudia, was having a great deal of trouble with one of her clients. The client had been verbally abusive on several occasions and had also made some very unpleasant personal remarks that Claudia was very upset about. As Claudia had to continue working with this client, she was understandably beginning to dread having to meet this client again.

One day, Claudia was in her office, sorting through some paperwork just before her lunch break when she was surprised by a sudden very strong surge of fear with a racing heart and dizziness. She happened to look at the clock and noticed that it was 12.00 p.m. The fear, together with all its physical symptoms, gradually abated, but nevertheless it left Claudia worried.

Being a therapist, Claudia recognised this occurrence for what it was, namely a panic attack. She noticed that she started worrying that the same thing would happen again the next day at 12.00 p.m., so she decided to take action. When she was in her office the next day, she said out loud, 'Fine, let's have it then! But this time I'm going to record this panic attack on tape!' She got her tape recorder ready as she sat back in her chair, eyes firmly fixed on the clock. She kept repeating, 'Fine, let's have it then, punctually at 12.00 p.m., and I am going to record it all!'

Nothing happened at 12.00 p.m. and nothing has happened since. Claudia had got rid of her fear by challenging it.

FREE-FLOATING ANXIETY

This is a state of mind where you feel constantly worried and afraid, usually without being able to say why. You are afraid that you are not good enough, that you cannot cope with what the day brings, and any deviation from your daily routine becomes extraordinarily stressful. Anxiety frequently goes hand in hand with depression.

Anxiety is usually a sign that a number of things have gone wrong for you in the past or that you are currently in an untenable life situation. Psychological factors are mostly the reasons why people become anxious. However, anxiety can be made worse by allergies, by consuming too many acid-producing foods such as chocolates, sweets and other foods and drinks containing sugar. Equally, taking recreational drugs can leave you with anxiety and paranoia, even years after you have stopped taking them. If you have been suffering from anxiety for longer than six months, and especially if you don't know why, it is best to seek professional help and advice. Anxiety can severely mar your quality of life, so do not suffer longer than necessary!

Use the following positive thinking methods consistently for two weeks. If you do not experience relief from your symptoms, find a good therapist − ideally someone who is trained in brief therapy or hypnosis, or see a health kinesiologist.

Affirmations
− I can learn to remain calm and relaxed no matter what happens.
− With every day I am relaxing more and more as I am peacefully releasing feelings I no longer need or want.
− My inner strengths now come to the fore and help me regain a balanced outlook and inner peace.

Script
I am slowly beginning to regain my emotional balance. I can learn to stay calm and composed no matter what thoughts go through my mind. My whole being begins to wind down; I am getting more and more relaxed and calm inside. Things that used to upset me in the past, now just calm and relax me. The more they upset me in the past, the more they now calm and relax me. I am allowing any unwanted thoughts to leave my mind easily and peacefully. Just like everyone else, I have a right to look forward to the new day with happy anticipation. My fears dissolve into thin air and I enjoy feeling calmer and calmer each day. My breathing is easy and effortless, my body relaxes and my mind becomes focussed and strong. I am happy as I notice that I feel more positive with every day that goes by.

Scenario

Imagine that you are taking all your fear thoughts out of your mind. Now make a big bonfire with all your doubts, negative beliefs and fears. As you watch all these unwanted feelings burn to ashes, imagine filling your mind with calm thoughts about happiness, tranquillity and peace.

Tips and tricks

1. Always precede your script with a relaxation exercise. Use the Relaxation Script for this purpose (*see* page 90).

2. If you have been using the above affirmations, script and scenario for two weeks and you don't notice any improvements, seek professional help.

3. Make sure that you are breathing properly. Holding your breath because you are tense makes fear worse. Every so often check that your breathing is still flowing. Make sure you breathe out all the way. If need be, tuck in your tummy muscles to expel all the air.

4. Check what is going on in your head! You can virtually drive yourself 'mad' by allowing negative thoughts to run riot. When you find yourself drifting off into disaster-thinking, think '*Stop This Nonsense*' and busy yourself with something at home or in the office to divert your thoughts on to more constructive things.

5. When you are feeling particularly anxious, keep repeating the phrase 'It is amazing how well everything is going for me!' again and again in your mind. This may feel very peculiar to start with, because it is clearly the opposite of what you feel at the time, but remember that your subconscious mind is impressionable! If you keep repeating a positive phrase, it will eventually 'sink in' and lift your mood and this in turn lessens your anxiety.

DEPRESSION

Depression is a condition that is closely linked to anxiety. You could say that depression is a fear of life which can, in severe cases, be completely debilitating for the sufferer.

We distinguish between two types of depression:

- exogenous (from without)
- endogenous (from within)

If you suffer from an *exogenous depression*, it means that the depression has been caused by an outside event such as the death of a loved one, redundancy, having failed an important exam, finding out that your parents want to divorce, and so on. These trauma causing events can be recent or from childhood. Exogenous depression usually responds well to therapy. *Endogenous depression* refers to a condition where there is no obvious external trigger for the feelings of melancholia. In these cases, it is assumed that there are biological factors that are the cause. Research suggests that low levels of the neurotransmitter norepinephrine in the brain is to blame, although it is not clear what causes these low levels. Patients with endogenous depression or clinical depression are often put on medication, although therapy can be an additional help. In my experience, the most successful course of action is treatment with health kinesiology.

Health kinesiology is used to help with both physical and psychological problems. It uses gentle forms of muscle testing to identify stresses on the individual's energy system. Once the stresses are identified, the kinesiologist holds various acupuncture points to bring the body back into balance so that it can heal itself. At other times, the practitioner will also place magnets on various areas to help the body overcome electromagnetic disturbances in the body system.

Depression or 'feeling low' is something we all experience at one stage or another in our lives. We might have to do things we don't enjoy which can trigger a drop in mood; we might be with someone who has a negative influence on our mood; the grey weather may get us down or we are overworked and feel depressed because we cannot see an end to the overload. We can also feel low because of a lack of self-esteem stemming from events in childhood, and in this case it is essential to sort these out with the help of a good counsellor or therapist.

Most of us are able to shake off the blues after a while. We either come to grips with the situation that is causing the depression or we find ways of resolving the situation to our advantage so that our mood can lift again. If we cannot come to terms with our situation nor resolve it, the depression can become a sitting tenant in our head.

When you are depressed, you are likely to display some or all of the following symptoms:

- crying
- loss of sense of humour
- insomnia
- negative thinking
- loss of sexual desire
- overeating or not eating at all
- eating lots of refined sugar
- fatigue
- hopelessness
- stress caused by everyday activities
- anxiousness
- anger
- going over past events over and over again
- helplessness
- not taking responsibility
- listlessness

Anxiety and sleeplessness, together with overeating or not eating at all, will deplete the body's energy reserves so that you are running on empty. The resulting fatigue turns any everyday task into a monumental issue, stressing you so that you get even more overwrought and hopeless.

Depression can be a result of something that happened in the past. Events that sparked off a strong feeling of guilt or inadequacy can (but do not have to) lead to a victim mentality where you feel helpless and overwhelmed by what is happening around you, even by the most mundane things. You may have been told what to do and what to think in the past, and now you are unable to think and act for yourself. As a consequence, the only things that are going around in your mind are *other people's negative comments about you*. You may just as well stay in bed all day . . .

If in the past your life has been run by others, it can become very difficult to take on responsibilities later in life – you simply don't know how to do it because you lack practice. In such a case you will probably feel overwhelmed by the prospect of having to deal with the world around you and make your own decisions. Some sufferers cannot sleep at night but spend a lot of the day in their room, cut off from the outside world, asleep. This is an inner-defence mechanism against perceived threats from the outside world – if I'm asleep, I don't have to deal with life.

One aspect of depression can be anger. If you have spent a lot of time in an environment where you were criticised, ignored or maltreated, either in childhood or later in life, you hurt inside. This inner hurt occurs when the criticisms happen, but often, people carry that hurt with them long after circumstances have changed and they have left the detrimental environment. A sign of unfinished emotional business is if you notice yourself regularly going over old incidents and still getting upset by the memory. When you feel hurt again and again, you start becoming 'allergic' to hurt and may develop aggressive feelings, not just towards those who have hurt you but also towards other people around you. Anger and resentment festers inside and is frequently offloaded on to friends and relatives who have nothing to do with the original cause of the hurt.

Depression can be a serious problem, and if you feel that your condition cannot be improved by self-help methods, then you need to get professional help. However, there is a lot you can do yourself to brighten up and become more resilient and positive.

Affirmations
- I am slowly beginning to learn to join the world around me again.
- I am important. My happiness is important. It can be achieved.
- I can do a little thing today which helps me become stronger.

Script
I am gradually beginning to change my focus of attention from inside me to the outside world. I am beginning to see things around me with a new sense of calmness and interest. I am beginning to understand that my life only has a purpose if I *give* it a purpose. I am starting to do little things for myself because I am worth it. I sit comfortably because I am worth it. I make myself a hot drink because I am worth it. I am as important as everyone else, no matter what people used to say to me. I am as important as everyone else, no matter how people have treated me in the past. My life is slowly beginning to change for the better. I am allowed to find things difficult and still conduct myself with dignity. I am allowed to make mistakes and still conduct myself with dignity. From today on, I treat myself with care and consideration because I am just as important as everyone else. I am a human being and I treat myself as a human being. I am important and my well-being and happiness are worth striving for.

Scenario
Imagine what the following emotions would feel like: happy, glad, fulfilled, delighted, tickled pink, overjoyed. Look at each word in turn, then close your eyes and think about that feeling. Repeat this exercise three times a day.

Tips and tricks

1. If you suffer from severe depression, you need to see a doctor and/or a psychotherapist. Use this book as complementary support while you are receiving professional treatment.

2. When you catch yourself thinking about yourself in a derogatory way, correct the thought immediately by re-phrasing it. For example, if you are thinking 'I am useless!' change it to something like 'I'm feeling very sad at the moment, but I can still achieve a little something for myself right now.'

3. Leave the house for ten minutes at least once a day, even if there is nothing you need from outside. By moving about you are exercising the body very gently and this in turn has a positive effect on your mood.

4. Make a point of saying something to someone while you are outside the house. A simple greeting and a short conversation will do.

5. Give your body some support during your depression. A homeopath can prescribe remedies that will help your body and your mind.

6. An important nutrient for helping with depression is tryptophan, an essential amino acid component of protein. Without sufficient tryptophan, the brain does not produce enough serotonin, a neurotransmitter that makes you feel good. Tryptophan is found in dried skimmed milk, beef, lamb, pork, cheese, pumpkin seeds, poultry, cashew nuts, peanuts, beans, herrings and eggs.

GUILT

Guilt is an inner prison where you are both the prisoner and the jailor. Guilt can keep you immobilised for your entire life; it can make you ill and it can distort all other aspects of your life. Guilt can affect your ability to have successful relationships with friends or family, it spoils those things that are good in your life and obstructs you from getting on with things.

Apart from causing depression and anxiety, guilt can also hinder your personal growth. The passage of time is an insignificant factor when you feel guilty. No matter how long ago you made your mistake, you can still feel awful about it twenty years later.

There are mainly three reasons why people feel guilty:

1. They have omitted to do something they should have done, for example, because:

- they did not help someone even though they could have
- they did not help someone because they were unaware the other person needed help
- they did not put the necessary work in to succeed at something and consequently failed or performed not as well as they could have
- they did not do what they considered to be their duty

2. They did something they should not have done, for example, because:

- they hurt someone else with words or deeds
- they were dishonest or stole something

3. They made a mistake, for example, because:

- they handled something in an inappropriate way through inexperience
- they made an inappropriate or wrong decision
- they damaged something accidentally

A guilty conscience is a useful warning signal when we have hurt someone with words, actions or inactions. It reminds us that we have to apologise and make amends in other ways. However, guilt should not develop into a life sentence.

The sad thing is that others may be able to see that we could not help making a certain mistake or that there were valid reasons why we failed, and they can try and reassure us, but as long as we do not forgive ourselves, we are stuck in our inner prison. Where we would show understanding and lenience if our best friend were to make the same mistake, we are quite uncompromising with ourselves.

The question we need to ask ourselves is, 'Where did I learn to believe that I must not make any mistakes?' If you think back, you may find that this is the way you were brought up. Maybe one of your parents was very strict and nothing was ever good enough? Maybe you did not get recognition as a child unless you excelled at what you did? Here are some other reasons that make you overly self-critical:

- having difficult parents who were hard to please
- being ignored and trying to get approval via outstanding performance
- being told or shown by implication that you are not expected to do well
- feeling you have to make up for a parent's short-comings

The fact is that we are all human. Mistakes, errors and failure are part of life and we have to acknowledge this fact and learn to live with it. Things do not always go right on the first attempt. None of us does the right thing all the time. None of us is successful all the time. Of course we need to strive to improve ourselves throughout our lives, but this will be easier if we don't carry guilt, remorse and shame around like excess baggage. If others are allowed to fail sometimes, so are you. No double standards please!

Affirmations

- I recognise that I have done wrong and ask for forgiveness with all my heart.
- As I make good my mistake I am allowed to let go of my guilt.
- I breathe freely as I forgive myself my past mistakes.

Script

I am now letting go of my feelings of guilt. I can learn from my mistakes and integrate my new understanding into the reality of my everyday life. I am continuing to learn and I am continuing to grow. Just like everyone else, I am allowed to make mistakes. Mistakes are part of life. Wherever I can, I make up for my errors and mistakes in the past. This is my positive contribution towards letting go of my guilt. I am willing to work on myself to avoid similar mistakes and errors in future. I now leave the past behind and begin to live in the here and now. My experiences and mistakes help me develop to become a better person. I am now developing a positive attitude towards myself and others. I focus my attention on the present and build up a happy and contented future for myself.

Scenario

Imagine in your mind's eye how you are freeing yourself from shackles and chains on your hands and legs, striding forward confidently through a beautiful landscape toward a new destination.

Tips and tricks

1. Take responsibility for your actions. Apologise to the other person in a sincere way and assure them that you will do everything to avoid hurting them again.

2. What exactly went wrong? Clarify this question in your own mind and take the time to reflect on how you can make amends. Once you have made up for your mistake, you can allow yourself to walk away from the guilt.

3. If you can make up for the hurt you have inflicted on someone, don't make your contrition a life sentence! You need to move away from the guilt, otherwise the other person cannot forget about the past event either.

4. If it is no longer possible to make amends, either because it is genuinely too late or because the person concerned has died in the meantime, decide on a 'substitute-restitution'. Help or support someone else instead. Set a clear time limit for this task, carry it out and then let go of the guilt.

5. If you feel guilty about something but are unsure whether it was really your fault, close your eyes and imagine the event on your inner screen. Watch the event on the screen as an outsider. This makes it easier to determine whether you were indeed to blame.

6. You can also write down the guilt-inducing event in detail, but write it as if it happened to someone else. This is another good way of helping you to distance yourself from the event and assess more easily what went wrong.

Corinne's Story
Corinne, a French lady in her late thirties, had been married for six years and was very happy with her husband Pete. Previous to her marriage to Pete, she had lived in France where she had been married before. When her first marriage split up, Corinne returned to live with her parents who looked after Corinne's little son Pierre while Corinne was out working during the day. Her relationship with her parents had always been fraught and she did not really want them to look after her son, but she felt she had no other option. When Pierre was six years old, Corinne came over to England for work and decided to stay. Pierre was left to live with her parents. Two years later, Corinne met Pete and they got married. She went to see Pierre frequently and had him come over to stay with her several times a year,

and yet she could not shake off the feelings of guilt that accompanied her every day. She felt she had abandoned her son in pursuit of her own happiness and fulfilment. Corinne could not forgive herself. In addition, she had the problem of having become very overweight since arriving in England, but had so far been unable to shift it.

Corinne found it hard even to consider the possibility that her weight problem could have anything to do with her feelings of guilt. However, she had to admit that it had started when she had decided to come to England. Once she began to let go of her guilt and self-accusation, she was able to lose her excess weight.

ISOLATION

We now have a higher standard of living than ever before. This means that we can afford to buy more goods, go on longer or more expensive holidays and surround ourselves with things that give us pleasure and entertain us. In order to afford all this, we have to work hard. Even though for many of us the working hours are shorter today compared to fifty years ago, we are expected to produce and achieve more. The jobs that used to be available to someone with basic schooling now require GCSEs or even A-level qualifications. The competition for jobs has become fiercer and employers' expectations of applicants are higher.

We want the same, if not better, than our parents, and we certainly want better for our children, so the pressure is on us to achieve. The competitiveness and pace of life today means that there is less time to socialise and to relax. The person who wants to succeed has to be single-minded and dedicated. This means pushing yourself, often beyond what is good for body and mind. Basic needs such as good food and rest are often overridden so more working time can be crammed into the day.

Not only is this way of life unhealthy, but it is also isolating. If you don't have time for yourself, you have even less time for others. That is why computer shopping is so convenient: you just press a few buttons and then collapse into a chair in front of the television while what you needed to buy is automatically dispatched to you.

People often say that they 'strive' on stress. This may well be, but body and mind need a counterbalance to perpetual activity, and this counterbalance is *not* just a vigorous game of squash or a workout at the gym, but unhurried private association with other people. This is not only relaxing but provides a counterpoint to the modern day isolation of the individual. It is often only on holidays that we rediscover that there is more to life than work. On holiday, we start looking around and notice the world that surrounds us and the people in it. We have time to talk at length with those closest to us and re-establish our links with others. Being with other people, seeing them, hearing them, speaking to them about matters outside the 'achievement arena' is a fundamental human need, and we are in danger of forgetting this in our drive to achieve and provide ourselves with everyday necessities, possessions and entertainment.

One of the consequences of our isolation is a sense of loneliness and boredom.

LONELINESS

Loneliness is a state of mind. It is not the same thing as being alone. You can be very lonely with a partner and three children around you. Similarly, just because you are single does not mean that you have to feel lonely.

Affirmations
- I am beginning to connect with the people around me in a positive and satisfying way.
- I am a loveable person and I gradually and safely allow other people into my life.
- I treasure my ability to communicate and I use it to my best advantage.

Script

I am loveable and I have the ability to create a happy and fulfilled life to share with others. All the skills I need are already inside me; all I have to do is use them. I am allowing myself the pleasure of sharing my life with others, enjoying their company and making time for fellow human beings. I discover my own strengths and abilities as I work on establishing warm and personal relationships with those around me. I look forward to meeting new people and I am open to new encounters. My confidence grows every day and I begin to enjoy spending time in the company of others. I find other people interesting; they add a new and valuable dimension to my life. I can feel myself relaxing more and more as I provide myself with the fulfilling relationships I need.

Scenario

Imagine yourself in the company of one or several people who you feel close to. See in your mind's eye how you are laughing and joking together, having quiet in-depth discussions or going out together.

Tips and tricks

1. Spend as much time as possible with people who make you feel good and as little time as possible with those who make you feel uncomfortable or 'wrong'. Sift through your family and friends and assess honestly who is good for you and who isn't. If you must spend time with someone who drains you, reduce the amount of time you are together.

2. Don't wait for others to talk to you. Make an effort yourself and take the initiative. Invite a friendly neighbour in for a cup of tea or ring up a friend you have not seen in a long time.

3. Accept invitations!

4. Strive to become the sort of person you would find attractive as a friend. Get involved in an activity; develop a hobby. Your area of interest does not have to be something useful; it does, however, have to be fun for you to do. The more fun you have in life, the more fun you are to be with.

5. Dare to talk about your feelings to others. People who only ever listen are easily exploited as an agony aunt (or uncle). Your openness will encourage openness from others. This does not mean that you have to talk about intimate details of your life at the first encounter with another person. However, volunteering information about your job, family, your interests or your last holiday will open the door for the other person to relax and talk to you much more easily about themselves.

BOREDOM

Loneliness is one thing, but what about boredom? We are surrounded by entertainment technology inside and outside our home, and yet some people find it hard to know what to do with their spare time.

Maybe the problem is that we are so work-orientated today that there is no opportunity for us to explore areas outside the work and family arena. We are used to passive, high-tech entertainment we do not have to create ourselves. All we have to do is make the money to buy the entertainment. Often, the money we earn also buys us the *time* for pursuing interests outside work. What is often missing is the *active* ingredient in supplying ourselves with an interesting pastime.

There may also be a lack of flexibility that makes us stay with what we know already (such as cinema, theatre, concerts – all of them enjoyable but passive!) rather than exploring new territory. We tend to choose those leisure pursuits that we are reasonably sure we can do without making a fool of ourselves. This is a great shame because it means we go for things that are already familiar to us and therefore safe – and consequently less exciting.

Affirmations

- I am determined to add excitement to my life, and I am starting today.
- I am the best person to give meaning to my life. Only I can fulfil this important task.
- My life is made glorious by my exceptional ideas.

Script

From now on, I am taking responsibility for my own well-being. The time for boredom is over, the time for thrills is beginning now because I say so. I am now looking at life from different angles. I can now see things that I could not see before. I can now see things that I did not dare look at before. I can take small risks and enjoy the challenges which I set for myself. I am getting excited about my new ideas and about the interesting events that are coming my way. I am opening the door to a new world, a world that holds meaning, interest and fulfilment. New opportunities for fulfilment present themselves because I am looking for them, and I grab them with both hands.

Scenario

Start off with a feeling of happy expectation. You can create this feeling by remembering a time in the past when you felt pleasantly excited about things to come. If you have no such memories, *pretend* in your mind that you can feel happy excitement. Notice what images come to your mind. What are you thinking about that makes you feel happily excited? The images you are getting now will give you an idea of what you could do to feel more fulfilled in life.

Tips and tricks

1. Ask yourself the following: 'What would I do with my free time if I wasn't bothered about making a fool of myself?' Once you have answered this question, pretend that you don't care what other people think and go and do it.

2. If you are too scared or embarrassed to try out something new, see if a friend will go with you.

3. Be aware that you alone are responsible for your own well-being and entertainment. Don't blame it on others if you are bored. It is up to you to spice up your life.

4. Be prepared to get addicted to trying out new things. Initiative and motivation are invigorating and add zest to your performance in life, and they will also make you feel more content and in control.

5. You do not have to pursue extreme sports such as parachuting or free-climbing to feel excited. For some people, learning how to swim is all they need for weekly excitement. Always choose an option that is not way out and only just beyond your level of comfort. That way you are strengthening your confidence in small achievable steps.

OBSESSIONS

I remember a time when I lived in Germany and the Iron Curtain was still dividing East from West. Occasionally, a few privileged East German pensioners were allowed over to the West for a few days or weeks. When the pensioners saw a West German department store, they went haywire. For them, it came close to a miracle that you could buy virtually anything you wanted. Coming from the East where demand outstripped supply, they were used to queuing for hours just to buy toothpaste, shoes or meat. East Germans would buy sandals in winter because in summer there might not be any for sale. So when the East Germans came over to the West, they would for example buy a whole stack of assorted batteries to take home, revelling in the availability of everyday goods.

In the case of the East German visitors their urgency in buying goods was understandable, but our own shopping habits are not. Even though we live in a world were practically anything is available in our shops we still display a behaviour that suggests that we are in great need. Ten-year-olds 'need' new clothes and new gadgets all the time, and so do we adults. We seem forever to be shopping for clothes or gadgets, and in some people this becomes an obsession. They are driven by the desire to shop and often they no longer know what they already possess. In women, this is particularly the case with clothes and cosmetics; in men, it is often the latest technological gadgets. Wardrobes are full of unworn clothes, studies are filled with computers and technical accessories that are given away or thrown out in six months for a newer model. What is happening?

This obsession with shopping arises out of a sense of boredom and unfulfilled emotional needs. It is as if there is an emptiness inside which has to be filled with the urgent acquisition of goods so that the emotional hunger is temporarily satisfied. The behaviour and actions of a shopaholic are very similar to those of a binge eater. An urgent desire drives them to consume, but the satisfaction is only temporary and they are left with the same empty feeling and an additional burden of guilt once the consumption spree is over. And not only that: unless you are very rich, you can get yourself into serious financial trouble if you keep on comfort-buying. Similarly, if you binge-eat on a regular basis, you put on a lot of excess weight and this then leads to even greater dissatisfaction and further binge eating. A vicious circle.

But obsessions can show themselves in other ways too. With the genuine greater work stresses we have today, there is a real danger that we become work-obsessed. There are lots of people who have a big workload, but not all of them feel stressed by it, so there is clearly another component that comes into play. Sometimes it is simply a matter of bad time-management or the inability to structure priorities sensibly that causes undue stress, but obsessive overworking can be a mark of underlying depression (*see also* pages 61–5) or low self-esteem (*see also* pages 44–7).

Another reason why some people feel the need to overwork constantly is that they feel an urge to do everything to perfection. Understandably, this will make their lives very difficult because they will find it very hard to finish any work they are doing, be it at home or in the office, for fear of it not being good enough, with the added worry that others will judge them by their (perceived) mediocre performance.

EMPTINESS

When we are unfulfilled, we feel empty. When we feel empty, we go shopping. For some people, acquiring possessions is enjoyable and gives them satisfaction. This is quite different, however, from those who are amassing possessions in order to fill an inner emptiness. If the latter is the case, shopping is just a substitute for a lack of meaning in your life.

What is it that is causing the emptiness inside us in the first place? There are a number of reasons that can leave us unfulfilled:

- a dissatisfaction with our own person
- a dissatisfaction with our circumstances
- a lack of meaning in our lives

When we are dissatisfied with ourselves, we are very critical of our looks and/or our performance. We think about ourselves in harsh words and spend a lot of time abusing ourselves mentally. This negative and self-destructive pattern of behaviour has usually been learnt from parents or teachers and needs to be unlearnt before we can relax and be more contented with ourselves.

When you are dissatisfied with your circumstances, you can blame your parents, your partner or the current government. None of this will change your circumstances in the slightest. The responsibility lies entirely with you and it is your duty to yourself to do everything in your power to change your situation for the better.

When you feel unable to find meaning in the life you are leading at present, you either need to change your circumstances or you need to change your attitude towards yourself or your circumstances. If you cannot do either of these things or have already done them, then you need to *construct* a meaning for your life and attach it to the work you are doing. There is no rule that says that meaning falls like manna from heaven and is mysteriously revealed to you one day while you are mowing the lawn. We all have to create meaning by constructing our own images of the world around us. According to our current outlook, we *determine* what the meaning of our life can be for us. Meaning is an individual subjective experience and cannot be provided by another person. For this reason, it is also insufficient to make another person into the meaning of your life – this would still leave you incomplete. Shopping, in any case, is not the answer!

Affirmations
- I can learn to accept who I am and what I have. I am poised, gracious and strong.
- With every day I am becoming calmer and more at peace with myself.
- I am filled with purpose and determination to make my life meaningful and fulfilling.

Script
With every day I feel calmer and more in control. I am becoming aware of my breathing, my body, my self. I listen carefully to the thoughts that are occupying my mind during the day. I pay close attention to what my body and mind are telling me. I am beginning to take myself seriously and I speak in a calm and dignified manner with myself. I treat my person and my life with respect and consideration. At the same time, I begin to understand more and more what I need to feel fulfilled and contented, and every day I work on providing myself with some of these essential things. I am learning to love and respect myself.

Slowly I am beginning to understand what is important to me and as I discover my values and opinions, I can construct a meaning for my life that brings me fulfilment.

Scenario
Imagine what it would be like to feel contented. Fill your mind with the word 'content'; repeat it over and over and attempt to create the feeling of contentment inside yourself. It may sound peculiar, but you can actually access a feeling by dwelling on it frequently.

Tips and tricks
1. Make time every day to look in detail at the clothes or gadgets you have been buying recently. Spend at least five minutes looking at one of the newly acquired items. For example, with a skirt you have just bought, sit down and look at it. Try and describe in your mind exactly what colour it is. Look at how it is put together, the seams, the lining, the waistband. Now pick a top from your wardrobe that goes with the skirt. Again, look at it in great detail, touch it and try and describe the texture and colour in your mind. If gadgets are your passion, do a similar thing. Spend at least five minutes looking at every single detail on the gadget, the colour, the design, the overall size, the colour of the display. Dwell on this gadget and spend time looking at all the single details. This activity will help you appreciate what you have and make you pause for a little while. This, in turn, can help interrupt the obsessive acquisition of possessions.

2. Sort out things you no longer need or want. Make sure you give them to someone who can use them, for example a charity shop or the YMCA. Do not just throw them away.

3. Relax regularly every day. Sit down for ten minutes, close your eyes and listen to your breathing. Count every in-breath and every out-breath as a separate number. Count up to sixty.

Concentrate on your counting. This is a simple exercise to help you feel more grounded and in control.

OVERWORKING

In order to provide ourselves with all the possessions we want and which our children expect from us, we have to work, and we have to work hard. Nowadays, both parents in two-parent families are likely to work, often through necessity rather than choice. There are also more professional women today who want to work.

At times, it is easy to forget that there is life outside work. We can get into a situation where our work is running us rather than us running our work. This is why holidays and weekends off are of *crucial* importance. If you constantly work you begin to forget who you are and you become physically and emotionally lopsided. The body is in a state of 'fight or flight' most of the time and your emotions are only geared towards your work targets. Anything that disrupts your progress to the target is treated as intrusion.

However, we need time to play. The harder we work, the more important it is that we have time to play as well. Playing in this context means a relaxed, non-pressure activity that allows you to be creative and to enjoy yourself. Vigorous exercise at the gym, good as it may be for letting off steam, is *not* play. Play activities can be:

- playing with a pet
- playing cards or other games, alone or with others
- watching a comedy
- reading a book which has nothing to do with work
- having sex
- playing with children
- being silly
- not doing anything at all – just sitting and letting your mind roam freely over fond, happy or funny memories

We are not always in a position where we have full control over our work schedule or workload. However, it is important to take every opportunity to influence the amount of playtime we get. You know that you have a problem if you do not want playtime any more or, if when you get some free time, it makes you nervous and you don't know what to do with it. This is called being a workaholic. It is not good for you, and prolonged periods of obsessive working are detrimental to your emotional health. You may thrive on stress, but if you consistently overdose and continue working even when you are ill, you will be creating serious problems for yourself in the long run.

Affirmations
- I allow myself to take breaks. My body and mind are entitled to rest.
- I am slowly taking a calmer and more relaxed approach to work.
- I am beginning to work in a more peaceful way.

Script
I can learn to approach my work with calmness. I am now beginning to take control of my work in a quiet and concentrated way. My thought processes calm down slowly but surely and my thinking becomes clearer and more focussed. I am beginning to feel how pleasant it is to work efficiently in a calmer way and am gaining back control. It does me good to work and move more slowly and to allow myself small breaks. I can even allow myself to leave on time and that is OK, too. I am beginning to rediscover my ability to play and enjoy the pleasure this brings me. My inner composure helps me work more calmly and more efficiently, and I become more centred and balanced.

Scenario

Imagine yourself approaching your place of work slowly, how you are *calmly* and *thoroughly* checking what needs doing and then set about doing the work in a quiet and methodical fashion.

Tips and tricks

1. Ask yourself why you are obsessed with your work. Do you need to control others? Do you need to escape something in your life that you do not want to face? Do you have to prove to yourself or others that you can do it? Are you under pressure to afford your family a better standard of living? Whatever your reason, be aware that your obsessive work pattern isolates you from people around you and will eventually make you very lonely. Is it really worth it?

2. Is your obsession with work filling a gap in your life? If so, can you make moves to deal with that gap in a more constructive and fulfilling way?

3. Begin to reduce your working hours. Do so gradually to avoid the cold turkey syndrome where you suddenly panic because your life pattern has changed too radically too quickly. Reduce your working week by two or three hours to start with. Make sure you have a good 'gap filler' for these empty hours. Go to the cinema or just relax at home and listen to your favourite music.

4. If you are working seven days a week, take one day a week off, ideally a weekend day. If you have a family, your partner and children will appreciate you being around.

5. Do not take on any further work. Resist the temptation of filling your newly acquired free time with new projects.

PERFECTIONISM

You can be your own worst enemy if you are overcritical of your performance. Perfectionism is a sign of deep insecurity about yourself and the world around you, and it can be a side effect of depression. Women who have to have their house just so *all* the time rather than most of the time get anxious when everything is not in its proper place. Men who have to be perfectly dressed at all times, without fail and without exception, are having a similar problem.

With perfectionism in the workplace, you are unable to finish a piece of work because you constantly find another aspect that is not *quite* right. This makes it practically impossible to meet deadlines, and if you do reluctantly deliver your work by the deadline, you end up spending days afterwards in mental agony over the perceived inadequacy of your work.

Perfectionism is not healthy because it is not achievable and therefore it creates constant mental and emotional stress. Perfectionists are the prisoners of their own rules that do not allow for any flexibility or variation. Life, however, is not static; life fluctuates and we need to move along with it. The better we can adapt to life's ups and downs, the more in control we feel and the happier we can be. A perfectionist is trying to force his insecurities under control by setting rigid and absolute rules to adhere to. These rigid rules work nearly like a superstition: 'If only I stick to these rules, nothing bad will happen to me'.

If perfectionism is very severe and starts infringing on the sufferer's normal life, it is best to seek professional help. It is very likely that there is an underlying reason for the perfectionism and this needs to be sorted out before the problem can be resolved. In the meantime you can use the following suggestions as supportive measures or self-help techniques. I have aimed the following advice at someone who is overly critical of the work they do.

Affirmations
- Doing my best is good enough.
- I can learn to relax and do my work calmly and efficiently as best I can.
- I am getting calmer with every day and I am beginning to look at my work in a more constructive light.

Script

I am now releasing any tension from my thoughts and from my mind. I am letting go of what I no longer need and make space for peace and tranquillity in my mind. Just like everyone else, I have the right to live and work in peace. I am doing one thing at a time. I do my work calmly and efficiently and stay relaxed and happy while doing it. I am taking the liberty, just for a change, to do my work very well rather than perfectly. Very good is very good. It is perfect if my work is very good. I allow myself to be very happy with very good work. Small variations and minor unevenness in my work are permissible and acceptable. I am feeling so much better as I am relaxing comfortably while working, and minor variations in my work are quite OK. My inner feelings of harmony and tranquillity carry me through my working day in a most pleasant way. I am letting go of 'perfect' and I welcome 'very good' into my mind. I am losing all interest in agitation and stress; I am beginning to enjoy relaxation and peace of mind.

Scenario

Imagine you are working steadily and efficiently, checking your work *once* and then handing it in. See yourself content and smiling, and imagine what it would feel like to be satisfied after having completed your work.

Tips and tricks

1. Spend some time initially learning how to relax. Use the Relaxation Script (*see* page 90) several times a day and do your best, but do not under any circumstances do more than your best! Do the Relaxation Script frequently, but sloppily, and you will get the best results.

2. Learn to live with unimportant mistakes. Don't Tippex out an item on your shopping list that you misspelt or didn't write neatly. Just cross it out if you must and write down the correctly spelt word at the end of your list. Or just see what happens if you just leave it as it is . . .

3. Make sure you breathe properly. Breathe in so that your stomach rises, then let your stomach deflate as you exhale. While you are working, take a little break every once in a while and check that you are breathing correctly for five to six breaths.

4. Is there anything in your life at the moment that is causing you stress? If so, is there anything you can do to change it? If there is, get on with it and stop procrastinating.

5. Work on being truly yourself. That is the only person you can ever be convincingly. If you feel stuck, get professional help.

Marion's Story

Marion (35) came to see me because she was obsessed by the thought that she would harm her baby. It was her first child and she was torn by feelings of guilt for having these thoughts and was desperate to assure me that she would never ever do anything to her baby. 'I really love my baby!' she kept saying again and again. But she was unable to rid herself of the thought that she might batter her child and she could not understand why she was thinking about these horrible things. She felt she was going mad.

It does not help to reassure someone who suffers from obsessive thoughts. There is nothing anyone can say to truly reassure an obsessive person, so I knew that we had to look at what was underlying Marion's obsession. In a number of analytical hypnotherapy sessions we explored what subconscious material caused this enormous emotional stress on Marion to produce these negative thoughts. It turned out that Marion had had a very unhappy and distressing time as a child, with a mother who had wanted a little boy and instead 'only' got a girl. Marion remembered far back into her childhood and recalled a distinct feeling that her mother disliked her. Having her own baby had brought back these old memories, together with a great deal of anger. This anger needed to be directed towards her uncaring mother, but as a child, Marion had never had an opportunity to do so and, later, she still did not dare. This suppressed anger emerged on the birth of her own child and was expressed as obsessive thoughts against her baby. Once we had worked through the issues concerning Marion's childhood experiences with her mother, she reported that the obsessive thoughts were becoming less and less frequent. When I saw Marion for her last session, she had not had any distressing thoughts for two weeks.

CHAPTER FOUR

Physical Health

The body is a truly magnificent work of art. Every single minute of our lives, whether we are awake or asleep, millions of body processes interact and connect with one another, keeping our system going. Not even the most sophisticated computer could ever hope to mimic the myriad complexities of the human body. Because our body serves us automatically, without us having to 'instruct' it consciously, we take it for granted. Until something goes wrong.

It is only when we get unwell that we start paying proper attention to our body. The easiest and most convenient way of kicking it back into action is to take tablets, but this is not always the best way. Tablets don't always work, and they mostly don't address the cause of the illness, only the symptoms.

International Labour Office (ILO) research shows increasing incidents of stress in the workplace. Maybe it is a sign of the times that we are so focussed on *achieving* and *doing* that we forget about *being*. Part of being is about keeping in touch with your body and being aware what signs it is giving you. If we constantly overwork and don't rest, we overload the body with stress and eventually we will suffer with the consequences. You spend the first part of your life ruining your health to make money, only to spend the money during the second part of your life, trying to get your health back. It doesn't make sense.

Throughout this chapter, we will look at a number of the health concerns prevalent today. In 1999, the most common symptoms that people sought help for were abdominal pain, headache, chest pain, back pain, breathing difficulties and diarrhoea. I find this trend reflected in my practice as a hypno-therapist and health kinesiologist. In addition, I have noticed an increase in clients presenting with digestive problems other than diarrhoea, as well as with skin ailments and general exhaustion. You will find these areas covered in this chapter, together with a section on addiction, an ever-growing problem in these stressful times.

With all the following physical problems, emotions also play a part. Emotions can either be the root cause of the illness (in which case we speak of a psychosomatic illness), or they can be influenced in a negative way by the physical problem. Health is always dependent on your state of mind, as emotions trigger body responses and body states trigger emotions. It is actually healthier to be happy. Unhappiness puts the body under stress. This is one reason why positive thinking works on so many levels – physically, emotionally and spiritually.

TENSION

With three out of ten employees in the UK experiencing stress-related health problems, this clearly needs to be our leading theme for this chapter, and the main physical component of stress is tension. As you get mentally uptight about the work you do, about family concerns or any other matters, the first thing your body does is to tighten up as if it had to ward off a physical blow. This muscular tension then leads to other changes in the physiology of the body, with hormonal levels becoming unbalanced and an increase in adrenalin. It makes good sense to learn how to reduce this physical tension so that the body can relax and get back into a healthy balance.

When you have been working hard over a prolonged period of time without adequate breaks or when you are in a difficult life situation, such as going through a divorce or having a child that is very ill, your body and mind can go into a kind of spasm. You are coping well, you are doing what is required efficiently, but you are no longer able to switch off and relax. Your body always feels slightly tense, your neck and shoulders ache and you notice that you grit your teeth both day and night. Psychological signs of tension are that you are becoming more dictatorial, stubborn, insistent and, at times, unreasonable. You may realise you are being stubborn and unreasonable but you still cannot stop yourself. You know you need to do something more for yourself when a good night's sleep no longer helps you snap out of the tension.

NOTE: As tension is a very common problem, I have written a combined Script/Scenario. This is referred to throughout the book as the Relaxation Script. You will often find that you need to do this Relaxation Script *first*, before going on with the script of other particular problem areas. You may therefore want to mark page 90 so the Relaxation Script is easier to find when you need it.

Affirmations
- I allow my body to sink into deep and peaceful relaxation.
- I am now ready to relax and let go. With every breath I take, I relax deeper.
- Slowly all the muscles and muscle fibres in my body relax and release and let go.

The Relaxation Script

As I am thinking about my feet, I can see in my mind's eye how all the muscles and all the muscle fibres begin to release and relax gently . . . As I am thinking about my calf muscles, I can see all the muscles and muscle fibres relax and smooth out and lengthen out . . . As I am thinking about my thighs, I can see all the long muscles and muscle fibres relaxing, smoothing out and going into their most comfortable resting position . . . My breathing helps me to drift into deeper and deeper relaxation . . . As I am thinking about my belly area, I can see all the muscles and muscle fibres relaxing and releasing, expanding and extending gently and easily . . . My body is light and free. My limbs feel comfortably heavy. As I am thinking about my chest, I can see all the muscles and muscle fibres relaxing, expanding and extending . . . My breathing is calm and regular; I feel at peace. As I am thinking about my hands, I can see all the muscles and muscle fibres begin to relax gently and easily, fingers relaxing, wrists comfortably loose . . . As I am thinking about my arms, I can see all the muscles and muscle fibres relax and release. I am sinking deeper and deeper into comfortable relaxation . . . As I am thinking about my shoulders, I can see all the muscles and muscle fibres relax and release, my shoulders sinking down and down and down. My body is light and free. My mind is calm and relaxed. Unwanted thoughts drift away like little white clouds in a summer sky and I am left calm and peaceful and relaxed.

Tips and tricks

1. To get the best effect from the Relaxation Script, record it on to a cassette, speaking calmly and slowly. Make sure you leave a pause where you find . . . in the script. When you listen to your tape, use a personal stereo to get the best effect. Listen with your eyes closed and visualise the muscle relaxation as best you can. Listen regularly.

2. While you are listening to your tape or if you do the Relaxation Script without the tape, make sure your clothes allow you to breathe easily. Turn off any sources of noise around you. If you need to do the exercise during the day, tell your family you need some peace and quiet for fifteen minutes and withdraw to the bedroom.

3. If you want to enhance your Relaxation Script, you can imagine being in an ideal holiday location – a beach, in the mountains, by the sea, on a meadow with flowers. Include all the senses in your holiday image: sight, sound and touch, taste, smell. If you imagine yourself on a beach, hear the lapping of the waves, feel the warmth of the sun on your skin, smell the briney seawater as it laps on the shore, and watch the fronds of palm trees waving above you. Other locations could be a boat on a little lake, a colourful garden surrounded by trees or a place you knew in childhood where you felt safe and comfortable.

4. The Relaxation Script is *the* most important exercise in the book, so please take some time to use it, ideally once every day for a week or ten days. It is easy to learn the sequence of muscle relaxation by heart, and you will notice that this exercise will make a significant difference to your state of mind as well as your physical well-being.

Later on in this chapter, you will find more specific health problems under the heading of 'stress', so once you have practised the Relaxation Script for a while, you can go straight to the stress section if you are having problems with hypertension or headaches.

PHYSICAL HEALTH PROBLEMS AND SOLUTIONS

ADDICTIONS

When we get physically hooked on a substance, it is always a sign that something in our life is out of sync. Alcohol, nicotine, recreational drugs and prescription pharmaceuticals are today part and parcel of many people's lives, and these habits cut through all strata of society, from rich to poor, from young to old. On the one hand, we seem to be more aware of health issues and keeping fit, but on the other hand we suffer this epidemic of substance abuse.

It is difficult to say whether this is a sign of the times or whether addictive behaviour has always played a role in people's lives. Where years ago people were getting high on laudanum and opium, we now have coke, E and too many G & Ts in the pub after work. Addictions are nothing new, but the extent to which we are afflicted with them is very worrying. With drug dealers cruising past primary schools and children as young as six or seven becoming addicted to glue sniffing, it is time to acknowledge that we have a serious problem on our hands.

What is it that makes so many people from all walks of life become hooked on a substance? A lot of it starts innocently enough. The proverbial cigarette behind the bike shed and the first sip from a vodka bottle may just be bravado and peer pressure. Trying out what it is like to smoke or drink alcohol is not the problem. The problem starts when the substance becomes a substitute for something that is missing in you or your life. The search for thrills and mind-expanding experiences is one reason for addiction. Another is using substances to avoid facing issues in your life. Addictions can also happen in a more passive way: you were genuinely ill and were prescribed pain killers to help you through the worst stages, only to find difficulties in letting go of the tablets after the pain has gone.

For some people, drugs have become part of their lifestyle. You come home from work and smoke some dope to relax, you go to a party and buy some E just as you would buy a drink, you psyche yourself up for another gruelling day at work by taking an upper. All this may be meant as an interim solution, an intermezzo, a lark, and for some it stays just that, but not for everybody. Why do some people lose control over their habit so that it controls them?

The answer lies in each individual person. There are certain personality types that are more prone to addictive behaviour than others, but one thing all addicts have in common is a fundamental unhappiness regarding some aspect of themselves. If the nature of this unhappiness was known to an outsider, it might be considered trivial, but if an individual cannot emotionally cope with a personal issue, this can eventually trigger an addiction. So how do you get out of an addiction, especially if it is a serious one?

It appears that the most effective way of conquering addiction is to find a purpose in life. This purpose often consists of some sort of challenge. In his book *The Grass Arena*, John Healey describes how he overcame his alcoholism by developing a keen interest in chess, which he learnt to play very well. A client of mine who had a severe drug addiction was able to come off the drugs by taking up running. It seems that once you can begin to focus your attention on something outside yourself which holds your interest for long enough to become involved in it, you thereby develop a purpose and a meaning for getting up the next day, other than servicing your addiction.

The following positive thinking suggestions are to support you in overcoming your dependency. They cannot, however, replace medical or clinical support.

Affirmations
- With all my sadness/fear/anguish, I can still find a worthwhile purpose for my life.
- I am paying myself respect.
- My senses are attracted by something fascinating outside my head.

Script

I can feel all my feelings and still function. The feelings that bother me can be there while I am looking outside myself. I am observing what is happening around me, and even though nothing catches my eye or my imagination for a while, I notice how more and more often there are unfamiliar objects and people and events which my mind latches on to in a curious and gratifying way. These objects and people and events lift me out of myself and show me a way forward into a happier future. As I begin to seek out those objects and people and events that catch my imagination, I register a new feeling of hope and warmth pervading my body and soul. And as I move towards my purpose in life, I am beginning to experience feelings of satisfaction and excitement that move me forward into a posi-tive direction. I can leave behind me what I no longer need or want.

Scenario

Imagine being a foetus in a loving and caring mother's womb. Imagine the warmth and safety of being enclosed by comforting darkness, with the gentle rocking of this loving mother's move-ments. Next, imagine being held in that loving mother's arms as a small baby, cradled and embraced by someone who really wants you. Next, imagine being held by the hand by that same loving mother as you are both walking along the street. Imagine this loving and caring mother being with you today, wherever you go, whatever you do.

Tips and tricks

1. When you imagine the scenario above, it might remind you of the fact that your real mother was in no way loving or caring, or it might remind you that she was not there at all, maybe because she died young or was not available for other reasons. It is important you do not use this exercise to dwell on past unhappiness. Instead, consciously create these new scenarios and stay with the feelings they evoke during the exercise. The positive images will eventually encourage positive feelings of safety and tranquillity.

2. Is there anything in your life now that puts you under pressure or makes you unhappy? Is there anything you can do about it? If there is, are you doing it? If you cannot remedy the situation on your own, can someone else help you?

3. You may find that you need professional psychological help to gain the strength to overcome your present addiction. This is OK. Only intelligent and responsible people go for psychotherapy, the others stay stuck and blame everyone else for their problems.

4. The amino acid glutamine can be useful in overcoming craving for alcohol or sugar. Glutamine is freely available in health food stores. Research has shown that 2–4g daily works well. Don't take amino acids with food. Leave at least thirty minutes between eating and taking the glutamine. You can also take it last thing before you go to bed.

ASTHMA

The ever-increasing pollution of our air through exhaust fumes and factory emissions, additives in foods and the increase in dust mites in our homes all contribute to the rise in the number of cases of asthma. Most sufferers are children, with more boys than girls being affected by it, but asthma can strike at any age.

When asthma occurs in children, it is almost always due to an allergy where the child is sensitive to artificial food colourings, flavourings and preservatives. An asthmatic child can also develop hay fever and eczema, conditions which often run in families.

When asthma starts at adult age, allergy is less frequently the cause. Instead it can develop as a result of a cold, bronchitis or infections of the upper respiratory tract.

An asthma attack can be very serious and should not be taken lightly. It can be triggered by any one of the following:

- emotional stress
- sudden vigorous exercise
- chest infections
- sudden laughter or coughing
- sudden changes in temperature
- smoke, paint fumes, chemicals, petrol and diesel emissions, gases
- furry pets
- smoking

Signs of an asthma attack are:

- tightness in the chest
- short gasping breaths
- wheezing
- unproductive coughs
- postural changes
- difficulty moving about
- anxiety
- inability to speak (danger sign!)

Asthma is a medical condition requiring medication. Do not suddenly stop taking the medication as this can be harmful. Use the following suggestions as a supportive measure.

Affirmations
- I am calm and relaxed. I breathe easily and effortlessly.
- My lungs are relaxing comfortably and I breathe out all the way.
- My breathing is becoming calmer and calmer and I am relaxing more and more.

Script
With each day I am becoming calmer and more relaxed. My relaxation deepens, both my body and mind are becoming more restful. I am relaxed and I am staying relaxed, no matter what happens. As my mind relaxes so my body relaxes, and this is helping all my air passages to open up comfortably so that my breath can flow easily in and out. I am breathing freely and I can feel the oxygen filling my lungs. I feel relaxed. I stay relaxed. I feel well. My chest opens up wide and relaxes. My breathing is free and easy and I feel comfortable while my breath streams easily into me and easily out of me. With each day I am feeling calmer and more comfortable. Things that used to upset me now just calm and relax me. I stay centred and in control and tackle any issues in peace and quiet, while my breath flows easily in and out.

Scenario
Imagine a centre of warmth in your abdominal area, just below your navel. Picture this warmth going down into your legs and up into your chest where it proceeds to dissolve any tensions, so that all the air passages are expanding and extending. At the same time, watch all the tension and tightness in your body flow out of the tips of your toes.

Tips and tricks
1. Asthma is a serious disease, and it can be fatal. If someone in your family has asthma, make sure you know where they keep their inhaler. If they have an attack and it seems worse than usual, do not hesitate to take them straight to hospital where help is available.

2. Turn off the heating in your bedroom before you go to bed. The heating creates air currents that waft dust mite droppings into the air, which you will then inadvertently breathe in while sleeping. These droppings are allergenic and can cause an asthma attack.

3. Have wooden or linoleum flooring in your bedroom and as few 'dust-gatherers' as possible.

4. There are anti-mite covers available today to put on your mattress.

5. Note down for a week everything you eat and drink, and observe closely when your asthma gets worse. There may be a connection between eating or drinking particular things and your asthma worsening.

6. Try and eat foods which contain no additives and remember that chemicals are also used in wine and beer. You may want to look for naturally produced wines and beers.

BACK PAIN

Back pain is a common problem today and can have a number of causes:

- bad posture
- damaged discs
- pressure on a nerve
- muscle spasm
- damaged ligaments
- injury
- postural abnormalities (such as scoliosis)
- misalignment of a joint
- inflammation of a joint
- arthritis

Back pain can lead to referred pain – pain which occurs in other parts of the body. In some cases, there is a problem with the back but the pain comes out in a different part of the body and this can lead to confusion. If, for example, there is a problem with the upper part of your back, you may experience pain in the front of your chest. Similarly, neck problems can cause headaches as well as pain in the arms and hands.

If you are having recurrent back problems, one of the most important things to do is to check that your posture is correct and that your body muscles are strong. To help you with these tasks, you can see an Alexander Technique teacher who will instruct you how to stand, walk and sit without putting undue pressure on your spine. In a Pilates class, you will be taught exercises which help strengthen various muscles in your body so that they can support your spine more efficiently. Both Alexander Technique and Pilates exercises can improve your back considerably. People who were unable to bend enough to pick up something from the floor become flexible again, and people whose movements were inhibited by back pain find that they become pain free and agile again. It is well worth the effort of doing the exercises to get rid of the pain and free up your range of movements!

Affirmations
- My spine is extending comfortably towards relaxation and health.
- Every muscle and every fibre in my body is now beginning to relax comfortably, and a soothing warmth spreads out through my back.
- Slowly and gently my back is beginning to feel more and more comfortable.

NOTE: in the following script, I am assuming one of your hands feels comfortable and free of pain. Should that not be the case, you may want to substitute the word 'hands' with 'feet', the word 'arms' with 'legs' and the word 'shoulders' with 'hips'. Lie down when doing the script.

Script

As I am aware of the discomfort in my back, I am also aware of all the comfortable feelings in my hands. I am now beginning to focus my attention on my comfortable hands and notice how truly comfortable they feel. My attention focusses more and more on that truly comfortable feeling, and I find that the knowledge of this comfort relaxes me very deeply, much more deeply than I ever thought possible. And as I am becoming increasingly aware of the comfortable feelings in my hands, I notice to my amazement and delight how these comfortable feelings begin to spread out gently and easily and effortlessly into my arms, and from my arms into my shoulders where I am now becoming aware of a soothing sense of well-being. And as these comfortable feelings are continuing to spread through my body they are beginning to wander down my back, very slowly, very gently, very soothingly. And as they do so, I can feel the discomfort in my back begin to dissolve, slowly and gently and soothingly. With every moment that goes by, my back feels more relaxed, more comfortable, more released. All the muscles and muscle fibres are releasing and relaxing and letting go.

Scenario

Imagine you could go inside your body and look around an area that feels comfortable (in our example your hands). Look around in your imagination and note what colour the arm is from the inside: pink or red or white. Touch the tissue in your imagination and notice whether it feels cool or warm, rough or smooth.

Now imagine going into the inside of the painful area of your back and check again. What colour is your back from the inside? Does the tissue feel cool or warm to the touch, rough or smooth? Get as much detail as you can.

Now begin to transform the painful area to look and feel the same way as the comfortable area. If the comfortable area is pink and the painful area red, imagine getting a pot of pink colour and paint the red area pink. If the painful area feels hot, put on some ice cubes to cool it down; if it feels rough, put a soothing balm on it in your imagination.

Tips and tricks

1. There is no way of getting around improving your posture and muscle tone if you suffer from back ache repeatedly, but there are some herbs which are helpful if you have problems with inflammations. Dandelion, willow and primula can help. Use them as liquid herbal extracts. A tea made from meadow-sweet is a good replacement for aspirin tablets.

2. To help speed up the healing of damaged tissues in the back, ginger tea will help, although it should be made from fresh ginger. Grate a few shreds into a cup of boiling water and let it stand for ten minutes, then strain it and drink the liquid only.

3. Mussel extracts and fish oil are good supplements to take if your back pain is caused by arthritis. Equally valuable is nettle tea, best made from dried leaves. Put a teaspoon of chopped leaves in a mug of boiling water and allow to stand for ten minutes before you drink it.

4. A good exercise for a frozen shoulder is the following, which I call the 'Squeeze-and-Breathe' exercise:

- Put your left hand under the centre of your ribcage and place your right hand on top of the left. Keep your hands flat and pull your elbows close to your body so you are hugging the sides of your torso with your lower arms.
- Breathe in deeply and push your body towards your hands while at the same time pushing your hands against your body. Hold your breath and push hard. The longer you can hold your breath and push the better.
- Release your breath and relax your hands.

- Repeat steps 1–3 three or four times and do the whole exercise three times a day.

Christine's Story

Christine (48) came to see me for a variety of health problems. Amongst other things, she had been suffering repeatedly from a frozen left shoulder. Even though she could use her left arm normally, the constant discomfort bothered her. When we explored this problem further, it turned out that the shoulder was fine so long as Christine's working schedule was not too hectic. However, once she got stressed, she could almost immediately feel her shoulder seize up. This gave me the clue I was looking for. Pain in the left shoulder can be referred pain from the lungs and the diaphragm. When Christine was stressed, she held her breath a lot and tightened up her belly area, and this resulted in the pain in her left shoulder. I showed Christine the Squeeze-and-Breathe exercise (*above*) and she practised it for a week. She consequently became more aware of her breathing when she was stressed and often managed to continue to breathe properly when she had a lot on. This helped her prevent her left shoulder from freezing. On the occasions when she did get too stressed and did not breathe properly, she was now able to 'de-freeze' her shoulder herself by doing the Squeeze-and-Breathe exercise.

DIGESTIVE PROBLEMS

Digestion is the process by which food is made soluble so that the body can use the nutrients. Most people assume that digestion starts in the stomach, but it starts much earlier – in the mouth. By chewing the food, you are breaking it down into smaller pieces. The better you chew the easier it is for the body to continue the digestive process throughout the length of the alimentary canal (the gut). Chewing stimulates the production of the digestive enzymes which break down the food further so it becomes soluble and can be absorbed through the walls of the alimentary canal into the bloodstream. The food is transported first to the liver and then to all the other cells of the body. Here it is *assimilated* – the cells take it in and make use of it to produce energy. Energy in turn is needed for growth and repair of tissue.

Most foods contain substances which cannot be digested. Humans, for example, produce no enzymes to digest the cellulose from plant cell walls. Cellulose and other indigestible materials are therefore passed out of the body as stool.

Along the alimentary canal, there are many different sections: the mouth, the stomach, the small intestine and the large intestine. Along that path, things can go wrong, either because we are putting in the wrong foods, which obstructs the smooth working of the bowels, or through illness, infection or psychological trauma.

CONSTIPATION

Constipation is a by-product of unhealthy eating and lack of exercise, but it can also be a result of emotional upset. If you feel you need to 'hold in' unpleasant feelings, it can have a negative effect on your digestion. Ideally, you should be passing stool at least once a day. If you can only go to the toilet every other day or even less frequently, or if you have to strain to pass stool, you suffer from constipation.

Affirmations

- I know I have the power to stimulate my digestion and I enjoy exercising my body.
- I am relaxing more and more and I let go of what I no longer need.
- I am adjusting my way of eating and enjoy the crisp, clean taste of healthy foods.

Script

I am setting things in motion. I change what needs changing. I get rid of what I no longer need and I tackle those things that are bothering me. Gradually, I am removing the obstacles in my life. I am becoming more and more active and I am building new inner strengths and resources which help me move forward in life. I enjoy utilising my inner strengths in positive and productive ways. As I activate my inner resources, my bowels react in a positive way. As I am becoming more active, so my bowel function is improving. As I am removing superfluous and detrimental foods from my eating, my bowels eliminate their waste more and more easily. I am now taking the lead in my life and refuse to procrastinate when important things need to be done. As I look after my own well-being, my gut becomes more active. I am beginning to empty my bowels every day easily and effortlessly. All my body processes are starting to work together in harmony and my healthy, strong body is supported by my healthy, strong mind.

Scenario
Imagine how the bowels are filled with water and fibre and observe in your mind's eye how these are mobilising the stool, how it is moved along and eliminated.

Tips and tricks
1. In order to help the stool stay moist and thereby support its elimination, drink lots of still water, at least one and a half to two litres a day, bottled or filtered.

2. If you are introducing bran into your diet, do so *slowly*. Start with one teaspoon, added to your breakfast cereal or live yoghurt. Do this for a week until you increase to two teaspoons, then three in the third week.

3. Introduce more fibre into your diet by replacing at least some of the white bread you eat with wholemeal. This will give you more insoluble fibre.

4. For water-soluble fibre, eat apples, pears and dates. If you can afford it, buy organic fruit.

DIARRHOEA

Diarrhoea is characterised by frequent, liquid bowel movements. An occasional bout of diarrhoea is nothing to worry about, but if it occurs frequently it may be a sign of an underlying illness requiring medical attention. Some foods, such as dried fruit, prunes, rhubarb or beer, can cause loose stools if taken in excessive quantities, and so can eating food that has gone off. In these cases, the diarrhoea will not usually last long, unless it is caused by food poisoning which is much more serious.

Severe diarrhoea over a prolonged period of time can be life-threatening because it causes dehydration, so it is essential to drink lots of water. If the diarrhoea persists for longer than two days you should consult your doctor so that any more serious causes of the problem can be excluded. These could be:

- Crohn's disease
- colitis
- diverticulitis
- IBS (see pages 107–9)
- thyroid problems

Diarrhoea can also be caused by emotional stress, and this possibility should not be neglected. You will recognise this quite easily if you keep a note of when your diarrhoea occurs. If it coincides with stress and if you are generally someone who reacts physically to stress by getting stomach cramps, headaches and the like, your diarrhoea is the physical manifestation of a psychological cause. The following affirmations, script and scenario refer to cases of diarrhoea that have psychosomatic causes.

Affirmations
- I am living this new day peacefully and calmly.
- No matter what happens, I stay calm and collected.
- My inner peace is solid.

Scripts

I can learn to go through life calmly and with dignity. I am now leaving the past behind and building my future on a solid basis of tranquillity and steadiness. I am beginning to recognise my inner strengths and I am starting to use them in the most positive and appropriate ways. I can feel my own solid centre developing inside me. This inner centre of calmness helps me change my circumstances for the better. I can slowly let go of my fears and gain calmness and strength. I am becoming more confident and self-assured. I am peaceful and strong. My calmness puts me back in control and I start every new day with confidence and happy anticipation. As I am getting emotionally calmer, my bowels slow down and come back into balance.

Scenario

Imagine how your digestive processes slow down. Picture the food going *slowly* into the stomach where it is *slowly* processed, wandering *slowly* down into the small intestine and on into the large intestine. Watch the nutrients of the foods go through the cell walls of the intestine into the blood stream, taking all the 'goodies' to the organs. Imagine how calm your bowels would feel if everything happened so slowly.

Tips and tricks

1. Eat and drink as slowly as possible. Sit down when you eat and don't do anything else except concentrate on the food in front of you. This means no TV, no reading, and no computer!

2. Stop running around trying to do ten things at the same time. Do one thing, concentrate fully on it and finish dealing with it before you start another task. Work steadily but without rushing. Have little breaks in-between, even if it is only for three minutes.

3. If you are very stressed, use the Relaxation Script (*see* page 90) *first* before using the diarrhoea script. It is of utmost importance that you learn to relax your body and mind if you want your gut to calm down. Relax regularly, ideally once a day. When your body is stressed by emotional problems it will need a while to let go of the tension that has accumulated. Once the beginnings of inner calmness begin to get through you will notice the beneficial effects on your bowels.

4. Remember to drink water to make up for the loss of fluid that occurs during diarrhoea. Children and the elderly are in particularly danger of getting dehydrated and this can be life threatening.

5. When you have a bout of diarrhoea, don't eat anything for twenty-four hours, then go on to bananas, boiled white rice, dry toast and grated apples, avoiding all dairy products.

6. After an acute bout of diarrhoea, your body will have lost some vitamins and minerals, in particular calcium, iron, zinc and B12. A nutritionist or kinesiologist will be able to advise you about the supplements you should take to redress the balance. Alternatively, take a good combination supplement containing these vitamins and minerals.

IBS

IBS is short for Irritable Bowel Syndrome. It describes a condition of bloating of the abdomen with severe pain and diarrhoea or alternating diarrhoea and constipation. It is a condition on the increase. The most common causes are food poisoning, repeated lengthy courses of antibiotics, and food intolerances and it is made worse by stress.

Affirmations

- A great sense of calm pervades my body and soothes and relaxes my bowels.
- Slowly and gently my body's own healing forces are beginning to relax all the muscles and all the fibres of my bowels.
- A sense of warmth and well-being flows through my body and mind, relaxing, relieving and soothing my entire being.

Script

I am relaxing more and more deeply with every moment that goes by. With every breath I take, I sink into deeper and more comfortable relaxation. My body is slowly beginning to settle down. It is slowly beginning to calm down, and the healing powers of my body are now beginning to work for me. Tensions are beginning to dissolve, slowly and gently, and I am getting more comfortable and more relaxed with every moment that ticks by. What was uncomfortable a moment ago now becomes comfortable. What was upset a moment ago now becomes calmer. My bowels are becoming calmer and calmer and a lovely peaceful feeling is beginning to fill my abdomen. I can breathe a sigh of relief: everything relaxes, releases and calms down. I am filled with peace, my body and mind are in harmony.

Scenario

Imagine going inside your body and 'repairing' your bowels. Picture yourself painting the insides of your bowels with a healing ointment which helps re-establish healthy bacteria in the gut.

Tips and tricks

1. If you have taken antibiotics in the past, it is very likely that this has something to do with your current bowel problems. In order to re-balance the intestinal flora, eat live yoghurt regularly (but *see* tip 2 below) or supplement your diet with capsules of *L. acidophilus* and *B. bifidum*.

2. Many sufferers of IBS have an allergy or intolerance to wheat or other cereals and dairy products. Consult a nutritionist or kinesiologist to find out if this is the case. Some people also have a problem with meat.

3. For a long time, bran has been recommended if you suffer from constipation. *Avoid it at all cost*, it will make your IBS worse!

4. Eat several smaller meals a day. This helps your gut process the food more easily and keeps at bay the unpleasant side effects of IBS, namely bloating and wind.

5. Drink lots of bottled or filtered still water during the day, at least a litre and a half – or more if you can. This keeps the stool soft and helps with the digestive process.

SKIN PROBLEMS

The skin is the largest organ of the body. It protects underlying tissues and organs from dirt, germs, injury and the harmful effects of strong sunlight. It is waterproof, controls the rate at which water is lost by evaporation from the body and helps regulate body temperature.

If skin and hair are not washed regularly, they collect dirt, dried sweat and loose dead skin cells. This all forms an ideal breeding ground for bacteria and fungi and these can cause all manner of health problems. In adult life, hormonal imbalances can also have a negative impact on the health and appearance of your skin.

But there are also a number of other factors determining how good your skin looks and feels, the most underrated of which is nutrition. Your skin is a mirror of what you are putting into your body. Just drinking enough water can make a very positive difference, as can eating more fresh fruit and vegetables and less fatty and sweet foods.

Another important factor with skin problems is allergies. When you have an allergy to something you eat or drink, or to some environmental substance which you come in contact with through touch or inhalation, this can make your skin come out 'in protest', so if you suffer from a skin complaint, make sure you have this aspect checked out as well.

ACNE

The hormonal changes that occur during puberty will affect about eighty per cent of teenagers by producing acne on their skin. In adolescence, an overproduction of sebum (skin oil) is triggered by androgens (male hormones) and this results in pimples and spots – the teenager curse of acne. The resulting emotional upset about these unsightly impurities puts the body under even more pressure which, in turn, prevents the skin from healing up as well as it could. Another contributing factor to adolescent acne is diet. With most teenagers this tends to be of very low quality and it often consists of fatty foods, such as burgers and chips, sweets and carbonated drinks full of sugar – and not a vegetable in sight!

Affirmations
- My skin is calming down and becomes clean and clear.
- My body is adapting comfortably to all the inner changes.
- I am getting calmer and more relaxed and allow my skin to heal.

Script
I am getting calmer and more comfortable with myself. My body's hormones are making all the necessary changes, gently and easily, so I can grow up. I am calm and relaxed as I allow my body to unfold and develop peacefully. All the muscles and organs in my body work together in perfect harmony. My feelings of inner peace have a soothing effect on my skin, and slowly the impurities are beginning to disappear. Every day my skin gets clearer and cleaner as my sebaceous glands come into balance and produce the *right* amount of oil. Eating healthily

helps my body work better. Impurities are flushed out of my system with the water I drink. I take pleasure in my new-found inner calmness and I am pleased to notice the positive changes in my skin. I am getting calmer and more relaxed with every day and treat my body and my skin with the respect they deserve. I am looking after my skin and enjoy noticing all the improvements that are happening each day.

Scenario
Imagine how the glands in your skin are beginning to decrease their production of oil and visualise how the spots and pustules begin to heal up until you can see your skin as clean and clear.

Tips and tricks
1.   The more sugar you eat, the easier it is for bacteria to live in and on your body. If your diet is also high in fat, you are making matters even worse for your skin. Both sugar and fat contain substances irritating to the skin. The increased secretion of sebum attracts dirt, and this in turn attracts bacteria. Cut down on sugar and fat in your diet. This means less chocolate, less sweets, less carbonated drinks, less fried foods, such as burgers and chips, and less crisps.

2.   Keep your skin clean. There are lots of products on the market for doing the job, but you can also simply use lemon juice and water for cleansing.

3.   Drink lots of water. Water helps flush out your system and gets rid of the toxins your body needs to eliminate. If possible, drink still bottled or filtered water.

4.   Make sure your body gets enough vitamin A, which you can get from eating carrots, apricots and mangos.

5.   Vitamin E is known to be good for the skin. You will find it in avocados, pumpkin seeds and sunflower seeds.

6. In order to guard against infections, eat citrus fruit for its vitamin C content and take a zinc supplement to help your skin.

7. Avoid dairy products, such as milk and cheese, and if you eat yoghurt, eat the live varieties containing beneficial bacteria which help the gut to stay balanced.

ALOPECIA

In the skin there are hair follicles, deep pits in which hairs grow. The shaft of a hair is formed at the base of a follicle by a root consisting of capillaries and dividing cells that quickly fill with keratin while the hair continues to grow. Every three or four years, hairs on the head stop growing and fall out. Soon afterwards, the hair is replaced by new growth from the same root. This is a natural process.

To an increasing extent today, people are losing their hair because of illness. Conditions such as alopecia areata (patchy hair loss), alopecia totalis (loss of all hair on the head), alopecia universalis (loss of all hair on the entire body) and alopecia androgenetica (diffuse hair loss where the scalp shines through) affect an increasing number of people. More and more women seem to be affected by these highly traumatic types of hair loss.

It is still not entirely clear what triggers alopecia. However, some connections can be made with the following factors:

- the contraceptive pill
- lack of zinc and/or B vitamins, especially folic acid, inositol, and biotin
- lack of silica
- childbirth
- menopause
- antibiotics
- vaccinations
- hereditary factors
- hormonal imbalances

In the case of alopecia androgenetica, the cause is hormonal and genetic. If you find a lot of hair on your pillow in the morning or when you are washing it, go and see an endocrinologist (hormone specialist). You may have a problem with the contraceptive pill or hormone replacement therapy you are on. For about a third of sufferers of alopecia areata, the condition rights itself without help after a few months. If it doesn't or the patches keep recurring, it will need attention. Treatments for alopecia vary from drugs (such as minoxidil and steroids) to irritants applied to the scalp. These treatments do sometimes help restore hair growth, but they may also have side effects.

Working at my practice, I have had good results with health kinesiology treatment for all these types of alopecia, even in cases where the client lost their hair many years ago. Chinese herbal treatment can also be successful, as can many other forms of alternative therapy. Ultimately, each sufferer has to decide for themselves whether they prefer to go for conventional drug therapy or for complementary medicine. There is a lot on offer today to help restore hair growth.

Affirmations
- I love and respect myself no matter what I look like.
- I am getting through this temporary problem with poise and dignity.
- I stand by myself through thick and thin and I look forward to re-growing all my hair.

Script
I am staying in touch with myself throughout this ordeal. I always remember who I am and I am aware of my fundamental worth as a woman/man and as a human being. I am actively and constructively looking for solutions and look forward to re-growing my hair again. I am strong and determined, I can get through this. I hold my head up high as I am walking along the street. My life goes on and I always make sure I'm looking my best. I am still the same person, and I am moving and talking and interacting just as I did before. While I am seeking

out the most positive solutions for my hair, I am continuing to relate to others and move about in the world with poise and dignity.

Scenario
Imagine watching hair growing out of your scalp as if you could see it under a microscope and in time-lapse motion.

Tips and tricks
1. Find out from an expert if you suffer from a vitamin or mineral deficiency. Anaemia (lack of iron) is something many alopecia sufferers have in common. Other substances which may be deficient in your body could be B vitamins, especially folic acid, inositol, biotin, pantothenic acid, and also the minerals zinc and copper. Any of these deficiencies can be easily corrected with supplements from health food shops. Rather than self-medicate, I would suggest you let a health expert advise you on the right quantities to take.

2. If you are a woman and your hair loss gets too bad, do consider buying a wig. Initially, this may feel like admitting defeat, but it isn't. You can always have a wig-burning party once your hair has grown back. In the meantime, you will feel more comfortable and more confident when you leave the house. If you are a man suffering hair loss, you can also choose to wear a wig, or you might decide you want to cut your hair very short instead of hiding the hair loss.

3. Many alopecia sufferers, particularly women, feel ashamed about their hair loss and try to keep it a secret. This is fine and your decision, but take into consideration that life will be easier if you don't have to be secretive about it. You are the same person with or without your hair, even though you may feel different inside.

Suzanne's Story

Suzanne (32) came to see me at my health kinesiology practice because, three years earlier, she had lost all the hair on her head and body, including her eyebrows and eyelashes. She had been having problems with her thyroid, and initially these had resulted in patchy hair loss. After an operation on her thyroid, the hair loss became worse. One morning, Suzanne woke up and found she had lost all her hair overnight.

When something in the body is not functioning properly, it will be reflected in the way a muscle reacts to gentle pressure. I checked what Suzanne's body needed by testing her arm muscle. Then, I began to correct these imbalances by holding various acupuncture points and placing magnets on her body to correct electromagnetic disturbances that would not allow the body to function properly. After ten sessions, Suzanne's eyelashes and pubic hair started re-growing, and after further sessions, the hair on her head also started to re-grow.

ECZEMA

Stress can trigger an outbreak of eczema but the main culprit is an allergy of one kind or another. There are a number of types of eczema. Atopic eczema is by far the most common form. It normally runs in families and is caused by one or more allergies. Another form is contact eczema/dermatitis which is caused when the skin gets in contact with substances such as nickel (in, for instance, costume jewellery, zips and coins), metals, bleaches and detergents, synthetic musk in aftershaves, soaps, shampoos, deodorants, hair dyes and so on.

When you suffer from eczema, the skin looks red and inflamed and has little blisters, usually around the back of the knees, elbows, eyes and mouth. The skin is dry and itchy and feels thick to the touch.

Affirmations
- My skin produces soothing moisture which travels to the surface to heal, balance and comfort.
- My skin is slowly becoming softer, healthier and more supple.
- My inner feelings of peace and harmony gradually transform my skin.

Script
My inner feelings of peace and harmony have a positive effect on my body. My breathing is calm and regular as my body and mind begin to relax more and more. As my body relaxes, so my skin becomes smooth. I am now programing my subconscious mind to start the healing process for my skin and to produce healthy new skin cells. My body's own healing powers are now beginning to work for me, reliably and effectively. Gradually, all the old skin cells are replaced by healthy new cells. My body is producing more and more moisture which makes the skin surface soft and supple. The old skin cells can now be shed to make space for new ones. Everything in my body now moves into a natural balance. Everything in my mind now moves into a comfortable perspective. My inner peaceful feelings benefit my skin. As I breathe in, I breathe in what I want. As I breathe out, I breathe out what I no longer need. My skin regenerates slowly and surely and becomes smooth and healthy.

Scenario
See in your mind's eye how the dry skin becomes detached from the surface and how new, pink, healthy skin takes its place. Imagine this process happening for every part of your body that is affected by eczema.

Tips and tricks
1. Keep moisturising your skin during the day. Carry a good moisturiser with you wherever you go. Make sure the moisturising lotion or cream is free of perfumes and allergens. Ideally, it should be organic, made from plants.

2. Drink lots of water to help keep your body moisturised from the inside.

3. See a nutritionist or kinesiologist to find out whether you suffer from a food allergy as this can exacerbate your eczema.

4. To find out yourself whether you have a food allergy, exclude the following from your diet:

- cow's milk products
- eggs
- artificial additives and sweeteners
- red meat and processed meats
- smoked fish and shellfish
- potatoes, onions, aubergines, sweet corn, sweet peppers, chillies, tomatoes
- citrus fruit and juices
- wheat, oats, barley, rye, maize
- vegetable oil margarine
- tea, coffee, fruit squashes, alcohol, tap water
- chocolate and carob
- yeast, spices, herbs

Avoid these foods for two weeks, then start reintroducing them one by one. Try each food for two days. If your condition worsens, stop the food immediately and wait for another four weeks before reintroducing it again.

5. Foods that are helpful when you have eczema are green leafy vegetables, root vegetables and fruit (except for citrus fruit), oily fish, avocados, olive and linseed oils, pumpkin seeds (for their high zinc content).

6. Supplement your diet with 5g of evening primrose oil daily for four weeks, then 3g for eight weeks, then continue with a maintenance of 2g daily.

PSORIASIS

Psoriasis is a disorder of the outer layer of the skin. It mainly affects the scalp, back and arms and appears as thickened red blotches with a scaly surface. In normal skin, the dead surface cells are shed and the next layer of cells adapt to take their place on the surface, to be replaced by fresh living cells from still deeper in the skin. New cells are formed in the deeper layer as fast as dead cells are shed, so that the thickness of the skin remains constant. In psoriasis, new cells are formed more quickly than dead cells are shed so that the skin becomes too thick.

Only people with a hereditary disposition suffer from psoriasis. Possible causes for a flare-up of this skin condition include:

- alcohol consumption
- emotional stress
- sluggish liver function
- fruit and vegetable deficiency in the diet
- excessive amounts of cholesterol

Affirmations
- My feelings slow down and my skin cells slow down.
- I turn my loving attention to my body and help it heal itself.
- I *can* look after my nutrition and I can make a difference to my skin.

Script
My whole being is slowly becoming more comfortable, more at ease. I now begin to turn my attention to my body's needs and make some beneficial changes to help my body heal itself. My body knows how to make healthy skin. My body knows how to produce fresh skin cells at the right speed, at the right time. I am now helping my body regain the right balance and achieve a smooth healthy surface again. Gently, the outer layers of my skin are being let go, as the inner layers are soothed and calmed by the right nutrients. Slowly, my skin begins to calm down. Slowly, the fresh new layers of cells are being formed

in rhythm with the old layers being shed. The rhythms in my body begin to synchronise, slow down and work together, gently and easily and effortlessly. My skin can heal. My body is whole.

Scenario

Imagine you could go into the affected parts of your skin. Picture yourself spreading a soothing ointment over the new skin cells that are growing too fast. Imagine the ointment calming down the cells so that they slow down their growth activity. Picture in your mind how the cells multiply more and more slowly, until they are in time with the surface cells shedding.

Tips and tricks

1. Lecithin has been found to be very helpful in reducing psoriasis symptoms, sometimes clearing them altogether. Good food sources of lecithin are fish, eggs, peanuts and soya beans. Fish oils or flax seed oil should be taken daily. Linoleic acid and gamma-linolenic acid (GLA) can also be helpful.

2. Keep your diet low on meat and dairy products and this will help keep saturated fat levels down. As the blood cholesterol levels come down, the psoriasis will begin to clear.

3. Make sure you do not have a wheat allergy. If you do, cut out wheat flour from your diet.

4. Eat plenty of fruit and vegetables to improve your liver function so it can produce its own lecithin. Orange, red and dark-green vegetables and fruit are also good because they contain beta-carotene. The body can convert this into vitamin A which helps in the normal development of tissue.

EXHAUSTION

It is one thing to be tired after a long day's work; it is quite a different matter to be exhausted. When you know the cause for your tiredness, for example if you have been overworking or very stressed by a particular situation, it makes sense to resolve the problems around your workload or your life situation. However, when you feel tired all the time without any obvious cause, you should investigate further. Here are some possible reasons for prolonged bouts of extreme fatigue:

- emotional problems (anxiety, depression)
- being in a detrimental relationship (with parents or partner; problems with children)
- anaemia
- low blood sugar
- Addison's disease (adrenal exhaustion)
- Insomnia
- ME (myalgic encephalomyelitis)

When great tiredness is allowed to continue unchecked for a long time, you run the risk of incurring serious health problems. Be responsible and deal with the underlying cause of your exhaustion if you know what it is. If you suffer from anxiety and this causes you tiredness, sort this out by seeing a psychotherapist. If you are hopelessly overworked, find out how you can work more efficiently and take more breaks or get some help in to take part of the pressure off you. If you don't know what is the matter, see your GP or a nutritionist and ask them to investigate further. You may simply need some supplements or a change in your eating habits in order to regain physical strength and alertness.

Exhaustion that has been building up over time cannot be overcome overnight. You will need to build up new energy slowly and resist the temptation to squander any small energy reserves you may have built up in one fell swoop. Use the rule of thumb that you should only do half of what you think you can do. If you use up all your energy at once, you will have to start again from scratch, so do a little work, then rest thoroughly before doing any more.

Tell others that you are unwell and unable to do the same amount of work you have been doing in the past. *Resist at all cost the temptation to do the work despite your exhaustion! If you do, you risk incurring serious health problems and possibly a breakdown.* The longer you postpone taking a rest, the worse your condition will get, and the longer it will take to come out of your exhaustion.

When you are exhausted, your body needs extra help. Here are some useful supplements:

- Take 250mg of vitamin C four times daily
- Take 50mg of pantothenic acid
- Take 1mg each of vitamin B2 and B6 or, if you cannot get these by themselves, buy a good B-complex.

Continue with these supplements until you see a marked improvement.

In order to help the recovery process, it is important to keep the lymph flowing around the body. Proper lymph flow ensures that the tissues are cleansed and unnecessary proteins and other debris are removed from the body. Unlike blood, which gets pumped around the body by the heart, lymph has no pump system to help it circulate. It is necessary to exercise the body to get the lymph flowing. Stretching is an ideal way of doing just that.

When you are exhausted, you can start with just one or two minutes of stretching a day. There are some simple exercises you can do to help yourself. If you are too unwell to stand up, you can do the first two exercises lying down.

Standing Stretch

- Stand with your feet together, toes pointing forward, big toes touching. Let your arms hang by your side, fingers pointing down. Keep your chin at a right angle to your neck, eyes straight ahead.
- Breathe normally and begin to lengthen your spine upwards while dropping your shoulders and stretching your arms and fingers downwards.
- Keep on breathing. While you listen to your breathing, hold the stretch for three or four breaths. Once you have a little more energy, hold the stretch for longer.

Stretching Up

- Stand with your feet together.
- Interlock your fingers behind your neck, elbows pointing outward.
- Breathe normally while you turn your palms upwards and push your arms up. Hold this stretch while at the same time lightly tightening your leg muscles. Don't lock your knees backwards, though. Hold the stretch for three or four breaths, longer once you have a little more energy.

Sitting Stretch

- Sit on the floor, legs in front of you. Place your hands on the floor next to you near your hips, fingers pointing forward.
- Breathe normally. Hitch up your toes and press your calves and thighs down into the floor. At the same time, stretch the trunk of your body upwards, as in the standing stretch. This may make your hands come off the floor, but that is OK. Once you are more flexible, you will be able to keep your hands on the floor.
- Keep on breathing and hold the stretch for three or four breaths, longer if you can.

PHYSICAL HEALTH

Case study

David (35) had been unwell since he was a child. If there was an illness going around, he was the first to catch it and the last to get over it. He was in and out of hospital with all sorts of illnesses. After years of back problems and lack of energy, David discovered hatha yoga where stretching is considered very important, with a strong emphasis on breathing correctly. Even though David is a slim person, he found it hard to believe how inflexible he was. 'I was never really interested in these contortions that some yogis can achieve, but just doing the basic stretches and eventually extending them has worked wonders for me. I have not been ill in years. Colds and infections seem to pass me by these days, and I have bundles of energy now!'

INSOMNIA

There are a variety of ways in which your sleep can be disturbed. You may find that it is difficult for you to fall asleep or you may find that you go to sleep quickly but then wake up several times during the night. This disrupted sleep then leaves you tired the next morning. Other insomnia sufferers find that they do go to sleep but wake up in the small hours, unable to go back to sleep.

Insomnia can be caused by anxiety or depression, but sleeplessness can also cause anxiety and depression. During the night, all the activity hormones are switched off so that the repair and growth hormones can get to work. Imagine your body is full of energy motorways which have hundreds of thousands of body processes driving along them during the day. If this activity continues throughout the night, the maintenance teams cannot do the necessary repairs which means that the energy motorways start deteriorating – your nerves become frayed because you are running on empty.

Good sleep is dependent on two factors: the state of your mind and the quality of your nutrition during the day. If any of these two components are out of sync, it can affect your

123

sleep – worrying keeps you awake, as do stimulants such as tea and coffee.

Affirmations

- Slowly my body and mind begin to relax into the deep comfort of my bed.
- All my thoughts begin to drift away like little white clouds in a summer sky, leaving me calm and peaceful and relaxed.
- I am completely calm and relaxed as my body enjoys peace and tranquillity flowing through my limbs.

Script

I am calm and relaxed as all my muscles and muscle fibres begin to expand and extend, sinking gently into the softness of my bed. My limbs are now peacefully releasing all the everyday tensions, and a feeling of warmth and well-being begins to flow through my body. My breathing is quiet and regular, relaxed and comfortable. I am drifting along on a feeling of peace and harmony. As I nestle my head into the pillow, a beautiful sense of relaxation pervades my body. I am becoming lighter and lighter as I am drifting along on a feeling of relaxation. I am light as a feather as I am drifting towards comfortable sleep. My eyelids feel heavier and heavier, my inner comfort becomes deeper and deeper. A wonderful feeling of peace and tranquillity flows through my body and mind. Like a little feather, I am drifting easily and comfortably towards deep and refreshing sleep. I am leaving the everyday world behind and drift into deeper and deeper sleep.

Scenario

Imagine yourself as a little feather that is drifting along on a warm evening breeze under the stars, drifting down and down on to a little stream which carries you along easily and effortlessly, between trees and grasses through the mild, balmy night.

Tips and tricks

1. Avoid alcohol. Even though a drink may initially relax you, it won't work on a long-term basis as alcohol is a depressant, and depression leads to insomnia.

2. Avoid tea and coffee, including their decaffeinated varieties. If you are sensitive to caffeine, even one cup in the morning can disrupt your sleep the following night.

3. Avoid having a nap during the day, as this will throw your sleeping rhythm out of balance.

4. If you have a partner, do not discuss any problems in bed. The bed is for sleeping, not for problem solving. Discuss problems before bedtime.

5. Make sure you eat enough during the day, but don't eat late. Hunger keeps you awake at night. If you are suffering from insomnia, don't go on a diet just now. If you are underweight, try and put on a few pounds – this will help you sleep better.

6. Foods that contain the sleep-inducing hormone serotonin are bananas, pineapples, walnuts and figs. Starchy foods like bread or malted milk drinks are also beneficial as they contain tryptophan, a precursor of serotonin.

7. Another remedy for sleeplessness is calcium. This is contained in Tissue Salt No. 1 (calcium fluoride), available from any health food store and some supermarkets. Take ten tablets before going to sleep and let them dissolve on your tongue. Often, this remedy works quickly and produces better sleep on the very first night. Keep taking the remedy for a while longer until the sleep problem has been resolved. If after three nights your sleep has not improved, increase the dose to twenty tablets.

ME (OR CHRONIC FATIGUE SYNDROME)

ME stands for myalgic encephalomyelitis, and this term describes its main symptoms: myalgia = muscle pain, encephalo = affecting the brain, myelitis = affecting the spinal cord and nerves.

ME is a condition where the sufferer experiences a debilitating lack of energy and muscle pain, accompanied by mood swings, depression and digestive problems. Even the slightest exertion can cause the sufferer to be 'knocked out' for several days, even though they may have felt fine performing the task at the time. The severity of ME can vary from day to day, sometimes even from hour to hour and this makes it difficult to lead a normal life. Not only do you feel desperately tired a lot of the time, but you also don't know how severe the symptoms will be the next day, so it is difficult to make plans. Possible causes for ME are:

- yeast overgrowth (candidiasis)
- viral infection
- amalgam fillings in teeth
- emotional stress
- vitamin and/or mineral deficiency
- inadequate detoxification by liver
- overuse of stimulants (alcohol, nicotine)
- food intolerances and allergies

Where you can, take away or reduce the stress your body is under. Stop smoking, cut out alcohol for the time being, have your amalgam fillings investigated and, ideally, replaced. See your doctor and check out whether you have a yeast overgrowth problem and, if so, have it treated. Have a general health check-up to see whether any of your inner organs are not functioning properly.

Affirmations
- I have a right to relax and rest.
- My body can now build up new energy reserves as I rest and relax.

– With every day, my energy reserves are replenished and strengthened.

Script

I can allow myself the time to let my body recover. Slowly and steadily the healing powers within me begin to re-establish a healthy balance between action and rest, rest and action. I am using my energy reserves wisely. I allow myself plenty of rest and I allow myself a slower pace, allowing my body to work efficiently and harmoniously. I treat my body with the respect it deserves. Nothing can disturb my inner peace. Others just have to wait, work just has to wait. My recovery is of paramount importance. My attention is now focussed on my physical health. My sleep is deep and refreshing, my body generates new energy while I am asleep. My energy returns slowly as I relax and rest, and I'm using my new found strength gently and prudently. Slowly, I am returning to everyday life. Calmly and wisely I deal with life in a relaxed and efficient way. My body's healing powers help me regain stamina, poise and flexibility.

Scenario

Imagine your body filling up with sparkling 'energy particles', swarming around and expanding into your limbs and your head, filling them with warmth and energy.

Tips and tricks

1. When you do your visualisation with the 'energy particles', you can create these in any shape you want. The important thing is that you see these particles as being packed with a strength so vibrant that the particles vibrate and shine. You can expand the scenario by picturing a strength reservoir in your body, which is being filled by the energy particles.

2. Exercise is fine, but only if it is gentle and slow. If you feel you can go for a walk for half an hour, only go for fifteen minutes. If you think you have enough energy to swim four lengths in the pool, do only two. Once your muscles are aching, you have already overdone it. Remember that any energy you can feel inside is filling up your reserve – the main tank is still empty!

3. If you find that candida is one of your problems, adjust your diet to exclude sweetened foods or foods and drinks high in natural sugars. Avoid bananas, fruit juice and dried fruit. Helpful in inhibiting the growth of yeast are onions, leeks, extra virgin olive oil, live soya yoghurt, and garlic.

4. Make sure you take 40mg of a good vitamin B complex as well as extra pantothenic acid (500mg) and the amino acid carnitine (250mg) every day to help your body recover. Magnesium has also been found to help with ME. Take 500mg chelated magnesium a day until there is an improvement, then lower the dosage to 300mg daily. Supplements of essential fatty acids in the form of evening primrose oil combined with fish oil are also helpful. Clinical trials have shown that 500mg of Efamol Marine eight times a day for three months showed marked improvements in eighty-five per cent of patients with post-viral fatigue.

STRESS

There are three different types of stress: emotional, physical and nutritional. Emotional stress can be caused, amongst other things, by:

- illness or disability
- bad relationships
- unemployment
- bereavement
- caring for a sick relative or partner
- being the victim of burglary, theft or mugging

- commuting
- divorce
- financial problems

Physical stress can be caused by:

- demanding physical work
- working long hours
- meeting tight deadlines
- insufficient rest and sleep

Nutritional stress can be caused by:

- caffeine
- sugary foods and drinks
- salt

All these factors can play a role in heightening stress levels and creating physical tension in the body. Read the section on tension at the beginning of this chapter, and also the Relaxation Script (see page 90). Two specific stress areas that are very common with the life style we are leading today are headaches and high blood pressure. Usually, there is much you can do yourself to help overcome these problems, provided you take a little care of your body's nutritional needs and make time to relax your body and mind regularly.

HEADACHES

When you have had a long night out and drunk plenty of alcohol, a headache the next morning will not come as a surprise. Similarly, if you have an allergy to wine or cheese and still consume these foods, you will know that you risk incurring a headache as a consequence. In women, another cause of headaches can be hormonal fluctuations before the onset of a period. In these cases, headaches are a nuisance, but they are harmless.

It is a different matter when you keep getting headaches without knowing why. The cause need not be anything serious, but you should consult your GP to have it checked out to eliminate the possibility. It is OK to take painkillers occasionally, but this is not a solution if your headaches keep coming back.

Affirmations
- My head begins to feel light and free and I feel better with every moment that goes by.
- Soothing and calming feelings flow through my body and my head.
- The tension in my head is now beginning to dissolve, leaving me calm, peaceful and relaxed.

Script
I am now allowing the tension in my head to slowly dissolve. Gently, all the tension in my head begins to smooth out and my life energies flow easily and effortlessly. Unwanted blockages dissolve gradually as I breathe calmly and regularly. With every breath I take, I am sinking into deeper relaxation. My whole body is relaxing, with my feet and legs smoothing out, my hands and arms heavy and comfortable and all the muscles and organs in my body working together in perfect harmony. Feelings of harmony and well-being flow through my stomach, leaving it warm and relaxed. I am allowing this healing, soothing warmth to travel gently upwards into my chest area, into my neck and throat and into my head. Slowly my head begins to clear until my head is left comfortable and soothed. I am feeling lighter and freer, my head is clear and calm. Any feelings that are superfluous can now leave my head and drift away, leaving me calm and relaxed.

Scenario
Imagine you could enter your head and find the area that is hurting. Picture yourself gently applying healing salve to the aching areas so that the pain is slowly soothed and eliminated.

Tips and tricks

1. Have your headaches checked out by a doctor if you are not sure why they occur.

2. Keep a headache diary, noting when your headaches occur. Write down what you have been eating and drinking that day, as well as where you are in your menstrual cycle. This diary can be very helpful in detecting the cause of your headaches, especially if a food allergy is the culprit or if hormonal fluctuations are involved.

3. If you find that it is emotional stress that gives you a headache, use the Relaxation Script (*see* page 90) first and follow it with the headache script.

4. Make sure you have your eyes tested. If you need to strain in order to focus on written material, this can cause headaches. Bad posture can also be to blame.

5. Peppermint applied externally to the temples in the form of a balm or oil can be helpful with tension headaches. Another natural remedy is Feverfew, a herb which should be taken as drops rather than tablets. Take 10–20 drops in a little water to help alleviate your headache. It should be taken for a few days or regularly if you suffer from headaches in conjunction with the menopause.

HIGH BLOOD PRESSURE (HYPERTENSION)

High blood pressure can sneak up on you without any clear outward signs, so if you know that you have a tendency to high blood pressure, it is a good idea to have it monitored regularly as hypertension, if unchecked, can cause heart disease, kidney failure and strokes.

Nicotine, caffeine and excess alcohol make your arteries constrict. This in turn causes your heart to have to work harder to pump blood around your body, and this results in your blood pressure rising. Prolonged high blood pressure can cause progressive damage to the artery walls. Please be aware that blood pressure medication does *not* cure the problem; only *you* can do that. This will involve some nutritional and life style changes.

Affirmations

- I am calm and relaxed and enjoy eating all the right things.
- My arteries begin to widen as I allow my body freedom from stimulants.
- I am taking pleasure in exercising my body gently. I can feel how moving my body makes me feel good.

Script

I am looking after my heart. My heart is the only one I have and it is the most important organ in my body. I am now giving my heart the respect it deserves. I relax regularly and enjoy the peaceful feelings which are beginning to flow through my body and mind. I am calm and collected no matter what happens. I am finding it easy and enjoyable to change to lighter, healthier foods. I find it easy to stay away from stimulants. Instead, I begin to prefer the crisp clean taste of healthy foods, fruits and vegetables. I feel lighter and freer as I move about more. I am enjoying recharging my energies as I climb stairs. I enjoy walking. I am moving about with pleasure. I am slowly and gently beginning to change my life style for the better and I take pride in my achievements. I am determined to make life easier for my heart. I am beginning to see the beneficial result of my positive life style changes. My strength and energy increase with every day and I have only myself to thank for these improvements.

Scenario

Imagine going into your body and watching the walls of your arteries widen so that your heart can push the blood through more easily.

Tips and tricks

1. Be aware that your blood pressure is directly linked to how hard your heart has to work. The higher the blood pressure the greater the effort for your heart to move blood around your body. Normal blood pressure is around 120/80. If you are regularly on 140/90 or higher, you are at risk of a stroke or heart attack.

2. Never stop blood pressure medication without your doctor's consent!

3. Change your eating habits. Avoid saturated animal fats and reduce your consumption of dairy products unless they are low fat. Avoid also high-sugar and high-fat bakery goods.

4. Take *gentle* exercise. If you cannot bring yourself to do some organised exercise in a class or in front of a video, walk more. Take the stairs instead of the lift and walk short distances rather than taking the car. Avoid aerobic classes; they are not what you need. Instead, go for gentle regular exercise such as the three stretching exercises (*see* page 122).

5. Restrict alcohol, nicotine and caffeine consumption as much as possible – ideally, give them up altogether.

WEIGHT

Weight seems to be the eternal problem for every woman in this world! Slim women are concerned that they are not slimmer, average and normal build women are worried that they are not thinner, and large women try everything to shed the excess pounds. This seems to confirm the American saying that you can never be rich enough or slim enough. Nowadays, even girls as young as six are worrying about their weight.

Another recent development has been that more and more men and boys have begun to look critically at their weight, so much so that there are now reports of cases of male anorexia.

The problem lies in the fact that we worry for the wrong reasons. We want to look a certain way, namely slim, because slim looks younger and fitter and slim is (at the moment at least) considered more sexually attractive. So the population spends millions of pounds on slimming aids, slimming clubs, slimming supplements and slimming diets.

It is perfectly all right to want to look your best. This is a sign of self-respect. However, what we should really be concerned about are the health implications of being overweight or underweight. (Let's not forget that there are also people who would love to *put on* weight, but are unable to add significant amounts.) If you cannot bring your weight down (or up) to an average level, something is out of sync. The body is designed to take nutrients from the food we eat and turn them into energy. This energy is used to help us walk and talk and work and play, but some of the energy is also used for digesting the food. If your digestion works well, wastes and toxins are safely excreted via the large intestine. If this waste disposal does not function properly, wastes and toxins remain in the body. These clog up the entire system, with more waste being accumulated as more food and drink is processed in the body. Imagine your household waste not being collected for weeks on end because the dustmen are on strike – this would soon become a major health hazard.

There are a great number of hormones and biochemicals involved in maintaining a healthy weight. It has recently been discovered that there is one hormone in particular, leptin, which helps the body regulate weight. When the fat cells in the body are full, they release leptin. Leptin tells the brain that there is no more need for hunger or appetite as there is sufficient fat in the body. However, in some people the brain does not understand what the leptin is saying and it keeps on producing appetite, even though there are remaining fat reserves. It is a bit like a foreign messenger arriving at the king's court, trying to convey an urgent piece of information, but the king does not understand the message. For quite a few people, a simple leptin correction carried out by a health kinesiologist has solved the problem.

Vera's Story

When I was seventeen years old, I had to undergo a course of treatment with steroids for a skin condition. As a consequence, I put on a lot of weight, mainly around my thighs and buttocks and this made my otherwise slim frame look out of proportion. No matter what I did, I could not shift this weight. If I did lose any weight, I ended up losing it from anywhere except from my thighs and I felt tired and looked haggard into the bargain.

During a seminar for health kinesiologists, Jane Thurnell-Read, one of the leading lights of the profession, introduced us to the solution. She had put together a test kit containing, amongst other things, a tiny little glass bottle of leptin. All you had to do was to put the leptin bottle on the client's abdomen and tap a number of acupuncture points. This, Jane explained, would help the brain understand what the leptin was saying (a rapid foreign language course for the king, so to speak!) and, hey presto, the weight would come off. And not only that, it would come off where you wanted it to!

Some of the delegates had already tried out this procedure and reported on their success. During the next break, everyone rushed to buy the test kit with the leptin, including myself – fat thighs and bum in mind! In the evening, we all went back to our hotel rooms and tested whether our bodies recognised the leptin or not. To my surprise, mine didn't, even though I am basically slim. That was good news as far as I was concerned. Slim thighs seemed within reach after thirty years. I put the leptin on my body and tapped the required acupuncture points.

The next morning at breakfast, I was getting ready to tuck into my breakfast. I have always needed a substantial breakfast to keep me going during the morning. I was somewhat confused when I found I was full up after half a slice of toast. I was now in conflict. On the one hand it looked as if the leptin was working, on the other hand I didn't trust my body to get me through four hours of seminar on half a slice of bread. In the end, I decided to go with what my body was telling me. I got through the morning without any problems and, over the next two weeks, ate a lot less than normal while still feeling perfectly energetic and healthy. Within three weeks I had lost ten pounds and, to my delight, I lost it off my thighs and bum! And even though I gradually began to eat normal portions again, the weight stayed off. If I have lots to eat one day, I feel full up the next day and *want* to eat less. Not because I feel I have to but because my body reacts that way.

I have consequently used this leptin correction on a number of clients and found that it works very well for about half of them, but not for the other half. Health kinesiology is clearly on to a very valuable solution to the problem of overweight, but more research is necessary which Jane Thurnell-Read is currently undertaking.

Weight is an emotional issue, and emotions govern your weight just as much as food. In my hypnotherapy practice, again and again I see how weight drops off once emotional issues are sorted out or, in case of underweight, weight is at last gained because eating habits and body metabolism change. Those clients who could not stop eating begin to eat sensibly. They report that they don't feel 'driven' to eat all the time. And, as they are more relaxed about eating, not only can they choose more carefully what foods they eat but also monitor better the *quality* of foods they consume. One of my clients said towards the end of his analytical hypnotherapy sessions, 'I feel so much more in control now. Because I am much calmer, I find I choose healthier foods, whereas before, I would just stuff myself with anything I could lay my hands on because I felt so desperate to eat.'

Clients who suffer from low weight seem to notice that they eat with more appetite and that what they eat 'sticks'. Having worked through an emotional issue appears to slow down their metabolism so that food doesn't just go in at the top and out the bottom. Greater emotional calmness results in better utilisation of food.

OVERWEIGHT

We know that crash diets are not a good idea because any weight you lose will be put back on immediately when you go back to your old ways of eating. Crash diets can slow down your metabolism so that after the diet you end up weighing *more* than you did before you started, even though you are not eating more. Your best bet is to eat more sensibly and this means reducing sugars and fat and increasing fruit and vegetables.

Affirmations

- I enjoy eating good foods calmly and attentively.
- I feel totally satisfied as I eat small portions of good food.
- I can let go of my excess pounds easily and effortlessly.

Script

My appetite is getting smaller and smaller with every day. I am unable to eat the same amounts I used to eat in the past. I feel calm and relaxed. Losing weight is amazingly easy. With every day my body is getting more used to feeling lighter and freer. Slowly I am shedding the excess pounds. With every day I am slimming a little bit more. I am beginning to feel lighter and freer. I am eating more calmly and I concentrate fully on what I am eating. I enjoy my food much more now than ever before. Even small portions leave me satisfied, completely satisfied. I can feel the *enough* feeling quite clearly and then I simply stop eating. I can even leave something on my plate and that is fine. I chew my food well and as I do, all the taste buds in my mouth enjoy the full flavour of the food. I can eat smaller amounts of good food and I am satisfied, completely satisfied.

Scenario

Imagine standing in front of a full-length mirror, wearing an outfit which is a size smaller. Turn to your right, turn to your left and notice how it fits you perfectly. Feel a sense of pride in your achievement and feel the great happiness of having lost the excess pounds.

Tips and tricks

1. For a week, each day write down *everything* you eat and drink, counting all the snacks in between as well as main meals and *all* drinks! You may be surprised at how much you really eat . . .

2. Only eat when you can concentrate on eating. Do not watch television, read or work while you are eating. You will eat less if you are aware that you are eating.

3. Do not eat over the sink, standing up or while you are walking around. Sit down and put whatever you are eating on a plate, even if it is only a biscuit. Never eat from packets.

4. Tidy away all foods in your kitchen. It is easier to grab something that is openly lying around, so avoid that temptation.

5. Avoid buying or storing sweets or chocolate. What is not in the house cannot be eaten.

6. Rather than going for an all-or-nothing diet, just change the balance between slimming foods and fattening ones. Adjust your eating (and drinking) to contain a lot more sensible foods and a lot less fattening foods. Allow yourself a daily treat.

7. Have some cooked food every day – eating only cold foods can increase depression and cravings.

8. Cooked oats help digestion and can also make soups more filling.

9. Fruit and vegetables will help your body lose water.

10. Sugary foods and drinks can be addictive. Avoid them as much as possible. Even worse than sugar are artificial sweeteners because they turn into formaldehyde in the body – a substance corpses are embalmed in! If you must eat sugar, eat the real thing.

11. Drink lots of water, ideally still mineral water. Water helps flush toxins out of the body, supports kidneys and liver and helps you shed the extra pounds faster.

Underweight

If you cannot put on weight even though you are eating sufficiently, it may be useful to have your doctor check out whether there is a physical cause such as a thyroid problem. Remember, though, that emotional stresses can also be a reason why you are unable to put on weight. If no physical cause can be found and there is no emotional stress in your life, you may want to go and see a health kinesiologist who can help bring your energies into balance on a subtle energy level, so that all the body systems can work together in harmony.

Affirmations
- I can eat calmly and peacefully and gradually I put on small amounts of weight.
- My body can learn to accept food and use it in beneficial ways.
- With every day I am becoming calmer. Anything untoward bounces off me and I am left calm and relaxed.

Script
My body and mind are beginning to slow down. As I continue to work efficiently, I am reacting more calmly to my environment. I am staying calm and relaxed no matter what happens around me. It is as if I had a protective layer around me letting

anything untoward bounce off me. I stay calm and relaxed and my attention is drawn more and more to food. I begin to discover more foods which I enjoy eating. To my surprise and delight I find that I can eat larger portions. My stomach is slowly accepting larger amounts of food. I am enjoying my food and my body accepts it gladly. The goodness from the food begins to settle comfortably in my body and slowly my weight gain becomes visible. I am pleased that the extra weight is showing in all the right places. I am calm and relaxed, and my calmness stays with me while I am eating. I take my time while eating. I breathe comfortably and eat as much as I am happy with.

Scenario

Imagine sitting in front of a big plate of delicious food, eating it calmly and with pleasure. Then imagine going inside your body and observing how the food is converted into tissue and thin layers of beneficial body fat, filling in all the areas that need to be filled in. Change to the outside again and imagine yourself in front of a mirror, noticing all the extra weight in all the right places.

Tips and tricks

1. Before you use the affirmations and script for underweight, use the Relaxation Script (*see* page 90) to help your body relax more deeply.

2. If at all possible, rest a little after eating. Leave the washing up until later and lie down for ten or fifteen minutes. As digestion takes up a lot of energy, you help your body preserve energy so it has more strength to metabolise the food.

3. Don't force yourself to eat foods only because they are high in calories. Just because something is fattening doesn't mean that it will be accepted by your body. Widening the variety of foods you eat while staying with good healthy foods is far better.

4. If you find it difficult to eat larger portions, eat more often. Never force yourself to eat more than feels comfortable. Forcing yourself creates stress, and stress will prevent you from putting on weight.

5. Weigh yourself not more than once or twice a week. Remember, every gram you put on counts!

CHAPTER FIVE

Relationships

Wherever people get together, there is the potential for conflict. Today, every third marriage ends in divorce. According to the UK government's Statistical Service, the percentage of single mothers and fathers has tripled over the last thirty years.

Communication

In good relationships there is little conflict and even that gets resolved amicably; in relationships where there is a lack of communication, misunderstandings and differences of opinion lead to rows and accusations. This goes on to put the relationship under strain. It is essential to communicate openly and in an appropriate way, not just in times of crisis but also in everyday life, but not everyone is willing or able to do so. This is equally true for professional as well as private relationships.

We can't change others, we can only change ourselves, and so it is important we learn to communicate well. When we communicate well we have better relationships with others, and this is why I have made this topic our main theme for this chapter. Good communication skills are vital if we want to keep our marriage or relationships happy and stress free. It is also important when it comes to dealing with everyday stress and the pressures of work, as well as the more traumatic events, such as the loss of a partner through divorce or death. Accepting your feelings and speaking about them will go a long way towards resolving the crisis for you.

What human beings want is to be loved. In order to be accepted by others, we need to be able to share our feelings, thoughts and opinions. If you are too shy to do so, you will find it hard to make friends or find a partner. You feel like an outsider and withdraw even further, making the situation worse for yourself.

Other people have problems because they communicate in an inappropriate way. They punish others by sulky silence if they don't get what they want, or they fly into a rage. If you can communicate well, it will put you at an advantage in life and will guarantee that you will have good relationships with others.

Affirmations
- I can speak easily and freely to those around me. Communicating with others gives me pleasure.
- With every day I become more relaxed about sharing my thoughts and experiences with others.
- As my enjoyment of communicating increases, my relationship with others comes into balance.

Script
I am allowed to feel comfortable within myself, I can feel relaxed and easy. My inner sense of harmony radiates around me and makes me communicate easily and effortlessly. I take pleasure in sharing my thoughts and experiences with others, and I take equal pleasure in listening attentively to their thoughts and experiences. I am open and receptive to receiving information from those around me, and I take great care to strive to understand thoroughly what they are telling me. I speak freely about my own concerns, as I want others to share my inner world in the most positive way. I am interested in those around me, and I want to help them get to know me, as much as I want to know and understand them. I speak easily and effortlessly and know that whatever we are speaking about enhances the bond between us, our love for one another and

our understanding. As I communicate, I learn and develop. I feel comfortable and relaxed and happy to have the opportunity to share my life with others.

Scenario
Imagine yourself speaking freely and calmly with your family and friends. Imagine a pleasant exchange of views and opinions. In this scenario, it is not essential to hear the actual words of the conversation in your mind. What counts is that you create a comfortable inner feeling which accompanies your visualisation of communicating successfully.

Tips and tricks
1. An excellent exercise to hone your communication skills with your partner is to speak about a topic that is important to both of you. Let your partner speak for one minute about his or her feelings about this topic and then repeat back to them what you thought they said. Your partner can give you feedback on whether your summary is correct. If it is not, they need to go over their points again for one minute, while you listen quietly and attentively. You then attempt again to summarise what they said. Only when your partner agrees that you understood correctly what they said to you do you get to speak for one minute about *your* opinion and feelings on this topic while your partner listens and then summarises your views. You will be surprised at how you hear what you *want* to hear rather than what is actually being said, especially if the topic is one of contention between you both!

2. Good communication includes speaking about trivia and everyday things. Communication needs to flow quite regularly between family members, friends and work colleagues on a daily basis while everything is going to plan. Only then can you communicate well when there are problems that need to be discussed. When you are monosyllabic on an everyday basis, you will find it impossible to speak easily and freely when a conflict

situation arises, simply because you lack practice and feel daunted at having to start speaking to the other party.

3. Communication does not just consist of speech. You can also give someone messages by the way you look at them, touch their arm or smile at them. Eye contact is also a very important means of 'being in touch' with someone. As you are looking at them while they are speaking to you, you show your interest in what they are saying. While you are speaking yourself, you can look away, but do come back to eye contact every once in a while to keep the rapport with the other person going.

With communication being our leading theme for the relationship section, please be sure to work through this section first before you go on to any of the other problems that are addressed in the rest of the section. As in all the other categories, the following issues are those that are most commonly experienced by us today.

RELATIONSHIP PROBLEMS AND SOLUTIONS

BEING SINGLE

We are leading more and more insular lives. With families frequently split up by divorce, single parents and single career people on the increase, social forecasters have estimated that by the year 2010, an extra five million homes will be needed to accommodate the rise in single living.

Even though singles have social contact with friends and colleagues, this is not the same thing as having a partner. Judging by the enormous number of lonely hearts ads and the increase in dating agencies, people still want to pair up, even if marriage is not necessarily the desired outcome. Maybe we are more cautious about marriage because of the high divorce rates and so prefer to just live together, but we still seem to prefer to be in a partnership than single.

The high divorce rates may be due to the fact that we have become more demanding and expect more from our relationships. At the beginning of the twentieth century, it would have been considered foolhardy, if not frivolous, to marry for love. If the man was a good provider and the woman a dutiful wife and doting mother, the marriage was considered to be a success. The fact that the husband womanised or beat his wife would not have been a good enough reason for a divorce. Today, we expect romance and we get divorced because of 'irreconcilable differences', which can mean that we have nothing to say to one another any more. Another reason for the high divorce rate may be that we don't choose carefully enough when we look for a partner and we get together with someone because we are desperate, because we want to get away from our parents or because we feel too insecure to be on our own. Clearly, none of these are good reasons. Usually, incompatibility becomes apparent during the first few weeks of a relationship, but if your hidden agenda behind wanting to get married is strong, you tend to negate these incompatibilities and go ahead with the marriage anyway. In these cases, divorce is the right thing to do. Sometimes it is necessary to leave the wrong partner in order to find the right one. At the same time, you need to ensure that you resolve your personal problems or you will end up making the same mistakes again when you choose your next partner.

Any separation is traumatic, whether you were married or just lived together. It is often underestimated how difficult it can be to split up, even if you have never lived together.

If you end a relationship where you have not lived together, you have the advantage of being able to withdraw into your own private space to lick your wounds without being constantly reminded of the problem by the presence of your ex. Nevertheless, the emotional pain is still there.

For children whose parents are separating or divorcing, the trauma can be nearly unbearable. As they are dependent on their parents, the shake-up of the parents' relationship induces severe existential fears in children. If adults find it hard to see a future while going through a divorce, it is ten times as bad for children, so it is particularly important for the parents to deal well with the situation.

Once a partner has left, there is not just the emotional upset you need to get to grips with, but also the fact that your life changes dramatically in other ways. Where you had a certain measure of companionship, merely by being in the presence of the other person, you now need to make your own entertainment. As a couple, you are socially 'invisible' when you go out to dinner, for a coffee or on holiday. As a single, you stand out when you sit at a restaurant table all by yourself. It takes special skills and a good measure of confidence to go out by yourself and feel comfortable about it.

And then there is the question of finding a new partner. This is not always easy, especially if you live on your own *and* work on your own. Many singles find it embarrassing to use a dating agency or put an ad in the papers. This is a great shame because what better place is there to find a partner than an agency where there is a constant supply of potential candidates for the man/woman-of-your-life?

DIVORCE (FOR PARENTS)

Even if a marriage has been on the rocks for a long time, it can still be traumatic when it finally comes to divorce proceedings. We know that divorce is one of the most stressful life events, especially when children are involved. Possessions have to be divided up and emotions run high when there are bad feelings about the separation. Divorce can truly bring out the worst in people, as disappointment, resentment and vindictiveness are openly vented. All this takes up a lot of emotional and physical energy for all parties involved.

Affirmations

- This too will pass!
- Every day brings me closer to a new beginning.
- I take every day as it comes and maintain my inner balance by focussing on the still centre in my mind.

Script

I can go through this divorce with inner strength. I make decisions calmly and to everyone's best advantage. With every day I am getting closer to a new life and a fresh start. Whatever is difficult today can be resolved tomorrow. Whatever holds me back today can be overcome tomorrow. It is OK for me to feel all my feelings. It is OK to feel all my feelings during the day and still sleep soundly at night. I sleep deeply and awake the next day, aware of my renewed strength. Feelings that bother me today become weaker tomorrow. I am calm and collected and I ride the tide like a cork on water. No matter how high the waves, I remain on top of things. Patiently, I ride the storm during the day and my batteries are recharged at night. With every day I become stronger and my inner strength helps me come to terms with the changes in my life. I can get used to my changed circumstances and soon I can go through life calmly and happily again.

Scenario

Imagine what you will feel like three years after your divorce. See all the problems long behind you, having established your new life, laughing again and leading your life the way you want to.

Tips and tricks

1. Don't cut yourself off from others while you are going through your divorce. Speak to your friends about your feelings. This will help diminish the emotional pressure, even if it is only temporarily. Having friends or relatives who listen is comforting and can often be helpful in finding solutions.

2. Try not to tell the same friends about the same trauma all the time. If you need a shoulder to cry on, make it a different one from time to time. And please be considerate. Even when you are feeling truly lousy, don't ring your friends in the middle of the night!

3. During divorce proceedings you may experience strong feelings of anger. This is normal. Make sure though that you do not make important decisions while you are in that mood. If you do, you can make mistakes that cost you dearly, emotionally and financially.

4. Don't take out your anger on others. It is not your children's fault that your husband/wife wants a divorce. When you feel like blowing your top, go swimming or jogging or rip weeds out in the garden until you are really tired. Any form of physical exercise can be a good way of letting off steam.

5. If you have no children and you are the one staying in the marital home after the divorce, it can be a good idea to make some changes. Put up new wallpaper in a room or two, reposition furniture and remove anything from your home that reminds you of your partner. Once the worst is over, changing your environment can help you change your thought patterns. If you can afford it, have a little holiday away from home to lift your spirits. Make sure you are not alone though – take a friend or go and see friends.

6. After a divorce or separation, you can easily feel lonely. It is now important that you have skin contact. Have a back massage or see a reflexologist. This will not only help relieve physical and emotional tension but also provide you with comforting skin contact. Frequent hugs from friends also do the trick!

DIVORCE (FOR CHILDREN)

When parents are separating, children become very frightened. All of a sudden, their sense of security and permanence is severely threatened and this means that their very existence seems jeopardised.

Here are some crucial points to remember when your children are going through your divorce with you:

- It is now very important that your children are talked to and allowed to show their feelings. Please do not make the mistake of thinking that children don't understand just because they are little. They do understand, so help them by explaining the situation to them in words that are appropriate to their age.
- Do not criticise your ex in front of the children. This will only make them more upset. If your ex is unreasonable, they will eventually find this out for themselves.
- Do not try and make out that your ex is a nice person when they clearly are not. If the children's father does not keep in touch with the children, do not invent excuses. If your ex will not let the children come on a holiday with you and the children ask you why not, encourage the children to ask their mother/father directly about it. In this way, your ex will become more aware that he/she is making the children suffer by his/her behaviour.

The following affirmations, script, scenario and tips are for your child. You may want to help by doing them with your child, or if your child is old enough they may want to read through the suggestions themselves and pick out what is useful to them.

Affirmations
- I am strong and I can get through this.
- I have courage and strength and I know that things can sort themselves out. I can be secure again one day.

– It is OK for me to have all these feelings and it is OK to talk about them.

Script

Whatever is difficult now is slowly becoming easier. Whatever hurts a lot now slowly begins to heal. Whatever is frightening now slowly becomes safer. I have a lion heart in myself which encourages me and gives me strength. I am carrying this lion heart with me wherever I go. It is firmly anchored in my body. My head is light and free, and I feel strong and confident. Everything is working out for the best. No matter whether I can see a way forward or not, I trust that everything is working out fine in the end. I take every day as it comes and look forward to a good and safe future for myself and everyone else in my family. Slowly my life goes back to normal and I can feel more and more peaceful inside. My lion heart carries me safely from day to day. No matter what happens, my lion heart protects and supports me. My future looks good and anything that is a problem now dissolves into thin air as time goes by. Everything turns out for the best in the end.

Scenario

Imagine you have a lion heart in your chest that makes you feel strong and courageous.

Tips and tricks

1. If you are lying awake at night worrying about the situation, speak to your parents and ask them what is happening and what their plans are. If you have sisters and brothers, get together and approach your parents together.

2. If you feel afraid or if you are really worried but cannot speak to your parents, you may find that there is a neighbour or a teacher at school who could help you.

3. If there are lots of rows between your parents, speak to one of them and tell them that this frightens you. Sometimes parents get so carried away that they forget that children can hear everything that is going on in the house.

4. Find out more about what it is like after a divorce. Talk to other kids at school whose parents are divorced and find out what it was like for them when their parents were separating.

5. If you find you are doing less well at school because your parents' divorce upsets you, speak to a teacher about it. When there is an atmosphere in a house because the parents don't get on or one of the parents has just left, it can be very hard for children to keep their attention on schoolwork.

LIVING AS A SINGLE PERSON

If you are single at the moment, you may not be very happy about it because you would much prefer being with a partner. Everyday pleasures can seem less enjoyable on your own. You may even feel you have to deny yourself certain treats like going to the cinema, to a club or on holiday simply because you cannot face going on your own. This of course takes lots of pleasures out of your life, so no wonder being single appears to you to be drab and joyless.

What most unhappy singles don't consider is that being on your own is a great chance in your life to:

- develop new skills
- get in touch with who you truly are
- please yourself
- do all those things that you will have less time for once you are in a relationship

Rather than bemoaning what you haven't got at the moment, look at all the advantages that you *have* got in your life right now!

Affirmations

- I enjoy using the time on my own to my benefit and advantage.
- My confidence grows daily as I claim more and more of the world around me for myself.
- I am determined to make this time of my life as happy and enjoyable as I can.

Script

I am delighted at having an opportunity to please myself. I enjoy doing exactly what I want to do. As I discover where my strengths lie, I begin to employ these strengths to discover new interests and develop new skills. It is invigorating to learn and it is elating to proceed. Even the smallest step of progress towards being happy as a single person fills me with pleasure. My happiness and interest in life and the world around me attracts other positive people. I am beginning to truly enjoy the freedom my single life affords me, and I provide myself with interesting things to do and exciting people to meet. I savour the privacy of being on my own and I delight in the company of new and old friends.

Scenario

Imagine yourself going out by yourself, for example to a café. Imagine yourself sitting comfortably, sipping a hot drink, reading the paper and looking and feeling perfectly comfortable and at ease.

Tips and tricks

1. Use your time as a single person to find a really interesting hobby. Sit down and close your eyes. Remember a time when you were happy and excited about something. Hang on to that positive feeling and think the word 'enjoyment'. Keep repeating the word in your mind while remaining with that positive inner feeling and see what images or ideas come to your mind.

2. Start conquering the world around you. Begin to practise going out on your own as well as with friends. Cinemas are easier than theatres and concerts because there are no breaks where you feel awkward standing around on your own. Cafés are easier than restaurants because you can take a paper and read while you are having a cappuccino. Start with the easiest task.

3. Stop feeling sorry for yourself and start living. Provide yourself with the happiness you deserve.

4. Don't wait for others to initiate events. Set up things to look forward to for yourself and invite others to join you. Remember, the happier you are the more attractive you become to others. Someone who is contented with their life can be more relaxed when meeting new people.

SHYNESS

Feeling unconfident in social situations is a big handicap when you are single. In order to make new friends and find a partner, you have to be able to relate to others so that they have an opportunity to get to know you.

Some people are shy because of past bad experiences, others have always been shy. Whatever the reason, you can still learn to be more outgoing and increase your chances of improving your social life.

Affirmations
- I attract nice people effortlessly and find it easy to chat with them.
- I can learn to speak to other people easily and confidently.
- I can learn to increase my confidence and look forward to spending happy times with new friends.

Script
I know that I can learn anything I need to live a happy and successful life. I am calm and relaxed and look forward to my

happy future. I can learn to move freely amongst people. I have a positive attitude; I am warm and open-minded. I am interested in others, in their ways of thinking and in their opinions. I look forward to discovering those people around me who share my views. I chat with lots of people and this helps me find out more about them. I can also speak about myself and about my own experiences in life. I like other people and other people like me. Slowly I extend my circle of friends. I am finding it easier and easier to talk to others. I attract nice people like a big magnet. I find more and more friends and my social life is really beginning to look up!

Scenario

Imagine yourself with others, laughing, joking and chatting. See yourself conversing effortlessly, with others listening and responding positively to your person.

Tips and tricks

1. Practise chatting. Start with simple tasks by greeting all those people who you know by sight with a friendly 'hello'. There is no need to stop and talk more – just walk past, make brief eye contact, say 'hello' and *smile*!

2. Once you feel more confident about greeting people, choose someone 'easy' and exchange a few sentences with them. You can, for example, ask them how they are and mention briefly where you are going. Have you got a lot of work on today or are you on your way to pick up your child from school? Do mention these things. Depending on the other person's answer, you can ask more questions or expand a little on your remarks. There is no need to chat for a long time, but make sure you don't just run off. Instead, say 'goodbye' and end the conversation with the words 'It has been nice talking to you.'

3. If you are not sure what to talk about, ask a question. Ask about the children or the husband/wife, what their holiday was like or ask for ideas where you could go on *your* holiday. Where did the other person enjoy spending time away from home? What in particular did they like about the location? Most people are pleased to give advice. *Listen carefully.* You often find that new conversation topics arise quite easily from what has just been said to you.

4. Speak to at least two people every day, no matter how briefly.

Anthony's Story

Anthony (19) was a clever young man but painfully shy. He went to university but didn't really enjoy his time there because he felt unable to join in with any of the social activities. Instead, he spent a lot of time in the library or studying in his room, but he felt he was losing out. His main problem was that he was afraid he would not know what to say in conversation.

In his sessions, we worked out a few scenarios for him to practise in his mind. His first scenario was to imagine that his pen did not work and he needed to borrow one off someone else during a lecture. Anthony did the Relaxation Script (*see* page 90) first so that he could go into his scenario in a calm frame of mind. He then visualised himself at a seminar, asking the person next to him for a pen. He practised mentally asking a young man and then asking a girl (which he found harder). He also tried out various different ways of asking until he found a way that felt most comfortable for him. His homework was to continue doing the relaxation and the mental scenario at home over the next week.

When he came back for his next session, he was beaming – he had already put his mental exercise into practice and it had worked very well. He got into conversation with a girl who had lent him a pen and they decided to do some of their revision together.

FINDING A PARTNER

It can be extremely disheartening when you are yearning for a relationship and there is no suitable partner on the horizon, nor any prospect of one. If on top of everything else you are also shy, it can feel as if you are bound to spend the rest of your life alone. But even if you are gregarious, it can be frustrating if the right person just doesn't seem to be amongst the people you meet.

Affirmations

- The right partner is already on his/her way to me.
- I am happy and confident while I am looking for my ideal partner.
- I look forward to spending a wonderful time on my own until I find my ideal partner.

Script

I am a loveable person and I look forward to a happy future with a wonderful partner. My happy and confident thoughts bring good things into my life and attract my ideal partner automatically. Every day brings me closer to my heart's desire. It is perfectly OK for me to take my time over finding the right person. I want the *right* person, not the *next* person. I am looking forward to a harmonious and happy relationship. I pursue my aim of finding the right partner happily and confidently. I feel relaxed, I like myself and I enjoy my life while I am looking. I take pleasure in meeting new people and finding out about them. I find it easy to talk about myself. I feel light and free, I am in a good mood and relaxed. My ideal partner is already on his/her way to me and when I meet him/her we will both know that we are right for one another.

Scenario

Imagine walking along the street hand in hand with your ideal partner, laughing and chatting.

Tips and tricks

1. Don't just dream – do something. Go out there to be seen. Don't hang out in front of your TV or computer every night, hoping that Claudia Schiffer or Brad Pitt will knock on your door to borrow your hairdryer! Join a club, go to places where there are other people, accept invitations. The more people you meet, the greater the likelihood that you will meet the right person.

2. Don't be put off by pessimists. Just because you are over forty-five, have children or don't look like a film star does not mean you won't find a partner. And another thing: disregard statistics that tell you that your chances are low at a certain age. There are lots of single people of all ages out there who are looking for a relationship, just like you do. I know people who were over fifty when they finally found their ideal partner. Anything can happen. Believe it and it will.

3. There is nothing worse than a desperate single person who is hoping to attract a new partner by incessantly talking *at* the object of their desire at a party. Relax, be happy, chatty, but don't move too close.

4. Use your time while you are still single and looking for a partner to turn yourself into a happy person. Make sure you look the best you can, work on your confidence if necessary, sort out the way you dress and present yourself. And above all, do all those things that you have always wanted to do. It is important that you have fun in life. The happier you are as a single, the wiser your choice of partner will be. Remember, it is up to *you* to provide happiness and interest in your life, so don't expect your new partner to make your life happy for you. They have to be right for you. If they are, they will enhance your happiness.

5.   Trust your feelings. When you meet someone who is single, *take your time to get to know them.* Try not to hop into bed with them straight away. Meet up a few times and check how you feel about them when you are *not* with them. If the thought of the other person makes you feel happy, pursue the relationship further. If you feel uncomfortable or doubtful, listen to this inner warning signal.

6.   There are no best places to find your ideal partner.

7.   Use agencies. They work for lots of people. They worked for me.

Barbara's Story
Barbara had always considered positive thinking to be a lot of nonsense, and she was going to prove it to everyone. She had been single for quite a while and was getting fed up with it, so she decided to 'order' a new boyfriend via an affirmation. He had to be dark and handsome and have a good income. She visualised this for just ten minutes, standing on her balcony in the evening. A week later she met a tall, dark, handsome and well-to-do young man. However, after half a year, the relationship broke off because they were not compatible.

Since the positive thinking had worked for her the first time around, Barbara visualised her new man again. This time she was more detailed in her visualisation. He had to like the same things she did, he had to look a certain way and be madly in love with her. A short time later, she met just such a man. They spent lovely times together, but in the end, it did not work out and they split up.

Finally, Barbara realised her mistake. She had to ask for the *right* man and not get lost in detail. This, too, happened, and she then proceeded to write a book about ordering what you want from the universe. The book went on to become a bestseller in her native Germany. A true story!

BEING A COUPLE

What is it that makes you a couple once you meet someone who you are interested in? The initial few meetings hardly qualify, although many women feel that once they have had sex with their partner, it means that they have a relationship with the man. Men would not necessarily see it this way, so we already have a discrepancy!

The fact that the man has agreed to see a woman more than once *and* has had sex with her often means to women that the man has agreed to a relationship when a better term for this status would be that the man is 'seeing' the woman. Working from the premise that the man wants a relationship with them, women then have expectations. They want phone calls, invitations to meet again soon, tokens of love, and any other sign that confirms that the man is very interested in them and that they are the special woman in his life. The man, on the other hand, may not have made a commitment to the woman at all — he is only 'seeing' her which to him means that he can ring up whenever he feels like it, expecting the woman to be interested in seeing him because she enjoys his company and his terrific sexual performance! It is not hard to imagine that all this can end with shattered dreams on the woman's part and confusion on the man's who does not understand why he is getting so much grief when he has never promised anything . . .

Two people, heterosexual or homosexual, become a couple when both have declared themselves openly to one another. This means that feelings of love are expressed in words by each of the partners and a mutual future is being openly agreed upon. If neither of these two points are met by *both* partners, they are 'going out' or 'seeing' one another, but they are not a couple.

COMMITMENT

Sometimes two people cannot become a couple because one of them does not want or is unable to commit to the relationship. Either the person is already married or in another relationship so that they are not really free to enter a new one, or the person is not really ready for commitment. The problem that now arises is that the missing commitment on one partner's side will not let the relationship advance any further. Both parties are stuck – one person is hoping against hope that the other person will commit while the other one will not or cannot do so.

If you are reading this as the person who *cannot* commit even though you want to, the best thing you can do is to get some professional help. If you are someone who does not *want* to commit and who is happy with this state of affairs, make sure you tell the other person that you don't plan to settle down with them. If you are the person who is waiting for someone else to commit to you, please note: *you are wasting your time.* You are in the process of making yourself very unhappy if you keep on waiting. The sooner you break away from your half-hearted partner, the sooner you will find someone who regards you as their special person. Someone who won't commit is bad for your emotional and physical health.

Affirmations
- I can let go of this unsatisfactory relationship and still stay intact.
- I deserve better.
- When it comes to a partner, I want a machine, not a spare-part!

Script
I can now allow myself to let go of someone who is incompatible with me. I have a lot to offer, I am a loveable person, and I am strong enough to walk away from hurt and pain. I value myself and I respect my needs. I am now beginning to walk away. Even though this hurts me, I know I can do it and I *am* doing it, right here and now. My happiness is of utmost importance to me and that is why I am walking away. I am now letting go of illusions and fantasies. I look honestly at what is, and what is not good enough. I treasure the time I had, but

now I am walking away. I am strong and I have self-respect and I am walking away with dignity. I am leaving behind what made me miserable and I am walking towards my future happiness.

Scenario
Remember all the times your partner has hurt you through their unwillingness or inability to commit to you.

Tips and tricks
1. Do not think for a second that you can change someone who does not want to commit to you.

2. Don't waste your time trying to understand a 'commitment-phobe'. All you need to know is that you are not their number one and you never will be. You cannot build your dream castle on a rubbish tip. Start walking!

3. Don't prolong the agony. Bring the relationship to an end as quickly as possible. You can ring or write a letter or you can use your next meeting to tell the other person face to face that it is over.

4. Stay polite and to the point when you announce your decision to split up. It is OK if your partner wants to discuss things, but do not be swayed by yet another promise to change. It is fair enough to give someone one or two chances, but after that, you need to be honest with yourself and realise that your partner is not going to commit to you.

5. Your partner may try and dissuade you from walking away by making out that *you* have a problem because you are impatient, narrow-minded, intolerant, neurotic or uptight. Agree with whatever they are calling you and then add that you still want to split up. And then start walking!

Sylvia's Story

Sylvia (33) had been working for several years at a school when their team was joined by a new male teacher. Just like Sylvia, John was single. They got on well, and soon a relationship developed. After only three dates, John told Sylvia that she was the love of his life and he was the happiest man on earth. Sylvia was in seventh heaven. Her ideal man had finally come into her life! They were both very busy with their school work so they could meet only rarely, but the summer holidays were just a few months away and Sylvia was looking forward to spending more time with John.

However, when the holiday break drew closer, it turned out that John had made plans to go away on his own, even though he kept assuring Sylvia that she was the love of his life. When Sylvia asked John why he had made holiday plans that did not involve her, John seemed surprised. He explained that a relationship could become boring if you spent too much time together and he thought it would be better to see one another only occasionally. Initially, Sylvia decided to accept this idea and waited to see how she would feel once John had returned from his holiday. He wrote a few postcards and rang her once or twice while he was away. On his return, he told her what a fabulous time he had had and about the interesting people he had met, mainly women it appeared . . .

Sylvia and John spent a lovely weekend together, but only two days later John announced he had enrolled in a sailing course abroad and was leaving for it in a few days time. Sylvia did not feel that John was really committed to their relationship. On the other hand, there were the lovely times they had when they were together. After talking things through with friends, she reluctantly decided that it was best to call it a day and told John so when he came back from his sailing course.

MOVING IN

Once a couple have declared themselves to one another and have decided that they want to stay together, the next natural step for many is to move in together. Living together is certainly more practical than living in separate homes – you save yourself constant commuting between each other's houses which involves carting clothes and other personal belongings from A to B. If you live a long way from one another and if you work long hours, moving in together makes sense.

What most couples don't realise to begin with is that moving in can bring its own problems. When you live on your own, you have everything in your home exactly the way you want it. Things have their specific order and place in the house, even though we may not be aware of our subconscious rules that govern this order. When someone else enters our space as a long-term or permanent companion, they will, of course, bring their own subconscious rules with them as to how to live in their private space, and their rules may very well clash with ours. Typical bones of contention include:

- what degree of untidiness is acceptable?
- how often should the flat be cleaned and by whom?
- can wet towels be left on the bed?
- can clothes be left lying on the floor?
- can friends and family come and stay overnight?

Some of these points may seem trivial but they can still cause friction between partners.

Another crucial question is, who will give up their own place and move in with their partner? Not every couple is willing or ready to invest in a new home together, so it is often the partner with more space available who stays put.

When you give up your own space to live with someone else, you give up quite a lot of individuality. After all, you come from a place where everything was yours. Most of your furniture will have to go because there will rarely be enough space at your partner's to accommodate any extra. And then there are all your clothes, books, music and other paraphernalia that have to go somewhere . . .

Cramming two people into a space that was previously occupied by one can create stresses on the relationship. Moving in together is a big change and needs to be handled well in order to work out for both parties. It is wise to plan as much as possible *before* you move in together, and clarify what each of you expect from one another when it comes to your living space.

Affirmations
- I adapt easily to the togetherness with my lovely partner.
- I enjoy negotiating, arranging and adapting to my new life.
- I am in harmony with my partner. Everything gets sorted out.

Script
I am aware every day that I have the privilege of being with my lovely partner. As we are now entering this new and exciting phase of our relationship, our love carries us forward in peace and harmony as we explore new ways of being together. I am willing and able to listen and observe, to communicate and compromise. My partner's happiness is important to me as is my own. I communicate easily and happily. I express myself in loving ways and enjoy the peaceful and considerate ways in which a mutual new order is established in our mutual space. I remember my love for my partner at all times, and this love helps me adapt quickly and easily to his/her presence. I also remember my love for myself at all times, and this love helps me express my needs and makes living with my partner a success for both of us.

Scenario
Imagine yourself being with your partner in your mutual home, doing things together happily, chatting and laughing.

Tips and tricks
1. Once you have *both* agreed that you want to live together, clarify which pieces of furniture can be brought in and how

space in the flat or house will be newly divided up to accommodate both your possessions.

2. Be prepared to compromise. Regard compromise as a sign of your love for your partner.

3. Expect your partner to compromise. Regard this as a sign of his/her love for you.

4. Establish household rules from the start. Clarify issues like cleaning, ironing, tidying, people visiting and so on, within the first two weeks.

5. Communicate, communicate, communicate!

6. If you don't get on living together, marriage won't cure the problem.

MARRIAGE

If you have already lived together before getting married, it will be of enormous help. Rules have already been established and you have 'test-run' your relationship. By now you will know that you are compatible and can live together happily. And yet, marriage is a big step into further commitment to the relationship in that you are making it public and legally binding.

When it was still socially unacceptable just to live together, marriage was a must for anyone who wanted to be considered a 'decent' person. Today, no one bats an eyelid if you are not married, so why bother? The answer may be that, for many people, the marriage ceremony has a deeper meaning than just living together. The formalised promise in front of witnesses of staying together and looking after one another in sickness and in health is a solemn occasion, rightly regarded as very important. It brings home to the partners that they are making a commitment for life.

Affirmations
- My husband/wife is the light of my life. Together we are strong.
- I enjoy all the good things that my marriage brings me.
- My love for my husband/wife brings out the best in me.

Script

I can relax for a moment and, as I am relaxing, I am thinking with great love about my husband/wife. I concentrate on all his/her good sides and I remember clearly all those times when [name of husband/wife] lavished these positive qualities on me. These beautiful memories allow all my loving feelings for my spouse to come up to the surface. I can feel positive emotions flowing through my body and mind, lifting me up and giving me strength and security. These strong positive feelings carry me safely forward in time and accompany me always, through thick and thin. I keep remembering occasions where [name] *said* just the right thing. I keep remembering occasions where [name] *did* just the right thing. My love for [name] becomes stronger every day. I feel sure and I feel strong and I find it easy to express my love towards [name]. The more I remember my husband's/wife's good qualities, the stronger our mutual bond becomes. I enjoy the warmth and companionship of our marriage and I become more and more aware how [name] appreciates my positive feelings towards him/her and returns them with love.

Scenario

Imagine a golden ribbon linking you to your husband/wife. See this ribbon becoming stronger and stronger. The ribbon comes from your heart and is attached to his/her heart. Warm and loving feelings flow along the ribbon.

Tips and tricks

1. The best guarantee for a good marriage is compatibility. You have to have the courage to leave the wrong partner (or *not* marry the wrong partner in the first place) in order to find the person with whom you can truly be happy.

2. Think back to what appealed to you about your husband/wife when you first started going out. Do they still have these good qualities? In times of crisis, make sure you concentrate on your partner's good qualities rather than just harp on about his/her less positive sides. If your partner is no longer displaying those good qualities, is there anything you can do to invite them back?

3. Do you *yourself* still have the good qualities that you had when you first got married? If not, you need to ask yourself whether you could not find a way of regaining them. Only when you can honestly say that you are doing everything to be an ideal partner yourself can you expect your husband/wife to be your ideal partner.

4. It is not always appropriate to continue a marriage. If your partner is violent, abusive or has a serious psychological problem and refuses to do something about it, it is better for you to separate. Divorce is traumatic for everyone involved, but a stressful end is better than stress without end.

5. Do remember that you can get help if your marriage is in crisis. A good marriage counsellor can help you resolve conflict and find solutions to problems that are putting a strain on your relationship. (*See* Useful Addresses, pages 235–7.)

6. Communicate, communicate, communicate. When something is bothering you, speak to your partner about it. Don't sulk, don't go silent, don't assume he/she can read your mind. If you allow something to fester it will eventually come out in a way that is too loud or too angry. Say what needs to be said while you are still in control. Say it calmly and politely, but say it. Invite your spouse to come up with a solution rather than be accusing or demanding.

Jane's Story

Jane (42) came to me for counselling sessions because she was unhappy in her marriage. She felt that her husband Pete was not giving her enough attention. They had been married for three years and Jane described the first year as having been very happy, with Pete coming home regularly in the evenings and spending all his time with her at weekends. However, two years ago Pete had been made redundant but had managed to start his own business. Initially, Jane had been supportive and understanding about Pete having to put in long hours, but she felt that the time had now come for him to take it easier and spend more time with her again. Pete claimed that this was not yet possible and Jane was angry about this. They started having rows with Jane accusing Pete of neglect and Pete claiming that Jane did not appreciate him.

When I asked Jane what had attracted her to Pete when they first met, she said it was his gentlemanly ways and the fact that he was considerate and looked after her by paying when they went out, ringing from the office when she was ill to see how she was, and generally making sure that she was all right. I explained to Jane that he was still looking after her today, and that working hard to build his business was his way of providing for her.

Jane realised that she had misinterpreted Pete's actions. She had assumed that he was more interested in his business than in his marriage. We constructed an affirmation for her that said 'I appreciate my marvellous husband and all he does for me.' After the session, Jane went straight home and told her husband just that. The result was that they started talking calmly about the situation and made plans for a holiday together. Their rows stopped.

Rows

Differences between partners are inevitable every once in a while, but when rows occur often, particularly if they escalate into shouting matches, it is time to reassess what is going wrong in the relationship. Check the following points:

- Are you saying clearly what you want?
- Do you know what you want yourself?
- Are you listening carefully to what your partner wants?
- Are you prepared for some give and take in your relationship or do you always want things your way?
- Are you really compatible or have you been rowing since the relationship started?
- Why are you still together if you row so much?

It is no good if only one of the partners wants to resolve a problem, so ideally, both of you should answer the above questions. Shouting is never the answer to anything, neither is name-calling or sulking. The only way you resolve a row is by talking about the matter calmly once you are clear what solutions *you* would find acceptable. Until you are sure what exactly it is that you want, you won't get your point across in a conversation with your partner.

Affirmations

- I can learn to express my opinion clearly and calmly.
- I can be constructive and find positive solutions to our differences.
- I am entitled to express my opinion and so is my partner.

Script

It is perfectly OK if my opinion differs from that of my partner. Differences of opinion can be talked through calmly and sorted out to everybody's satisfaction. Even if my partner finds it difficult to stay calm, I can. I am like a sturdy rock, reliable and strong. I stay calm and collected and keep the conversation to the point. I am focussed and I keep an open mind. I present my point dispassionately and calmly and I am prepared to listen to my partner with interest when he/she puts his/her point to me. I am conciliatory and want to bring the matter to a satisfying conclusion for both of us. It is important to me to avoid misunderstandings and I relate my point of view calmly and with clarity. I am honest in a kind and caring way. I am prepared to engage in our conversation until a solution has been found that suits us both. I am understanding and I expect my partner to be understanding. I express my wishes calmly and listen to my partner's wishes attentively and silently. Everything is finally working out all right. New ways forward become apparent as we speak, resolving the issue to our mutual satisfaction.

Scenario

Imagine yourself and your partner sitting down and calmly discussing a matter. It is not necessary for you to hear the actual words as long as you can see or feel yourself stay calm and collected even if your partner does not stay cool.

Tips and tricks

1. Never discuss important issues while you are on your way out of the door. Agree on a time for you both to sit down and talk. This also gives you the opportunity to think in more detail about what you want to say and what you hope the discussion will achieve.

2. Prepare mentally for your conversation. Be clear about what you want so that you can express yourself clearly when you speak to your partner. If you don't know what you want, you are unlikely to get what suits you. And don't try and hide your wishes behind a lot of words. Be polite but direct in expressing what you want.

3. Work on the premise that your partner is looking for a positive solution to the problem, unless experience has taught you otherwise. If your own attitude is positive when you enter a discussion, you are more likely to encounter positive reactions from your partner.

4. Try not to be thrown by personal remarks. Some discussions end in a row because one partner attacks the other verbally. The best way of dealing with this is to ignore it if you can. If this is not possible, agree with your partner ('Maybe I am selfish . . .') and then state your wish again ('. . . but I would still like you to help me with looking after the kids on the weekend.').

5. Don't buy into emotional blackmail or insinuations. Pretend you don't understand the underlying message and keep on negotiating for what you want.

DEATH

When you have been with your partner for some years, especially if you have spent a lifetime together and your partner dies, it will take you a long time to get over it. Irrespective of whether your partner was ill or died suddenly, the shock and grief are the same, even if you did not always see eye to eye.

For many parents, the death of a child is particularly painful because it seems against the natural order of things – it is the older generation that is supposed to die before the younger. For some, it takes years of pain and sadness before they can begin to come to grips with their loss. It is quite normal for the bereaved person to spend frequent periods during the day thinking about the person who died, even years afterwards. It is also normal and OK *not* to be upset about the death of someone who you did not get on with or who did you harm.

Affirmations
- I am allowed to feel all my feelings and I am also allowed to feel nothing.
- I now allow myself to let go of [name of the dead person] peacefully.

- I am connected to [name] in a loving way, no matter whether he/she is here or not.

Script

I am allowing myself to feel my grief. I am surrendering to my sadness and my forlorn feelings for a while. I am allowed to feel all my feelings and to openly express them. All my feelings are OK. All my feelings are valid. I am allowing myself to mourn as long as it is necessary. While I am sad, I can also feel happy when I remember all the good times we had together. These beautiful memories give me strength and comfort and help me overcome my despair. My grief lasts as long as is necessary to overcome my loss. It is OK for me to lean on others during this difficult time. It is OK to speak about [name of dead person]. Slowly, I am overcoming my grief. It is OK that my life is now changing from the way it was up to now. I can get used to this change and make the best of it. My grief is mine and I am safe when I allow myself to feel it. Slowly my pain begins to heal, and slowly I can take part in the world around me again.

Scenario

Imagine seeing the deceased person in a place of tranquillity and happiness where he/she is at peace.

Tips and tricks

1. It is perfectly normal if you find yourself talking to the dead person. There is nothing wrong with you, you are not going mad – quite the contrary. It can be a great relief to talk to the dead person in order to feel closer to them.

2. Feelings can be volatile during the grieving process. Anger and denial are as much part of it as is depression and numbness. Allow yourself to feel and talk about those feelings, even if you don't like some of the emotions that are welling up.

3. Don't let others dictate to you how long your personal grief should take. No one else can truly assess what your relationship with the deceased was like. The length of time you mourn depends on you, your personality and the relationship you had with the deceased.

4. If you feel you cannot cope with your grief and just talking to friends is not enough, get professional help or contact CRUSE (*see* Useful Addresses, pages 235–7).

5. Distract yourself from your grief every once in a while. See other people when you are feeling a little better or get busy with something outside the house in order to give your body and mind a bit of rest. Even though these distractions will only have marginal effects to start with, they are still helpful in that they temporarily lessen the impact of your grief.

SEX

The two classic topics for rows in a relationship are sex and money. Sex is the more difficult to resolve. If you need more money you can do some extra hours at work or get a second job; if you want more sex with your partner, you cannot just make them do it. In fact the harder you push for it, the less likely you are to get a willing or potent bed partner.

And what if you are beginning to realise that your sexual orientation is changing or not conforming to what society considers to be 'normal'?

SEXUAL PROBLEMS

It can be a great problem in a relationship if one of the partners experiences sexual difficulties. Both men and women can become temporarily impotent if they are under too much stress. If your body or mind is overworked, the body's pleasure centres shut down – men can't get an erection or cannot sustain it and women lose their interest in sex or become unable to have an orgasm.

For men, the situation is more difficult. They cannot pretend to go along with sex as women can, as men's 'performance' is physically visible. Also, men are psychologically vulnerable when their performance becomes below par. The fear of not performing satisfactorily puts them under pressure and produces apprehension and this is likely to make the problem even worse on the next occasion.

If stress is the reason for sexual problems, use the Relaxation Script (*see* page 90) before you start on the following script.

Affirmations
- I allow my mind to relax as my body's needs are met.
- As my mind calms down my body unfolds.
- I am allowing myself to let go.

Script
As I am relaxing more and more, my mind begins to calm down. I am feeling peaceful and comfortable as my thought processes begin to slow down. All the everyday worries are slowly ebbing away. I have all the time in the world to allow my thoughts and feelings to become calm and comfortable. Out of this mental calmness comes physical harmony. Out of the physical harmony arises a gentle pulsing sensation that I recognise and welcome. Calmly and happily I experience this joyful sensation. I stay passive as I sense the awakening of my body. My body and mind are focussed and begin to work in unison. My physical sensations begin to totally absorb my thoughts, and the focussed attention of my mind follows and reinforces my physical sensations. I can feel myself unfold harmoniously and with great pleasure.

Scenario
Imagine yourself having really good sex or, if you find this difficult, remember one time when sex was particularly good. Dwell on the image or the memory.

Tips and tricks

1. Sex can only work if you concentrate on it. When your mind is still on work issues or any problems you are experiencing at the moment, you lack the focus you need for sexual arousal. Being physically and mentally relaxed is one of the prerequisites for getting 'in the mood'. For this reason I strongly recommend you use the Relaxation Script (*see* page 90) *before* you continue with the sex script.

2. Remember that penetration is not the only enjoyable facet of sexual activity. If you are too tired to 'go all the way', you can still have a good time with gentle, intimate massage, touching and stroking. If you don't expect anything more, you often relax enough to become aroused after all.

3. If your sexual performance or libido is constantly under par because of stress, you need to look at your life style and your working habits. Does your body ever get a chance to recover from the everyday pressures? Are you subjecting your body to unhealthy foods, too much alcohol or nicotine? All this will sap your energies and affect your libido.

SEXUAL ORIENTATION

For those who are heterosexual and therefore conform to society's norms, it is reasonably easy to develop into sexual beings during puberty. When a teenage girl develops an interest in boys, the parents may sigh and feel exasperated about their daughter's waning interest in her schoolwork, but otherwise everything is OK. Everybody is curious to meet the boy she is going out with and the tacit understanding is that, eventually, their daughter will have sex. For the daughter, matters are similarly straightforward in principle. She feels an interest in boys and knows that she is considered 'normal' for wanting to pursue this interest. She may have to fight her parents for wanting to stay out late or for wanting to go out with a boy the parents deem unsuitable, but she does not encounter opposition about the gender of the person she is proposing to go out with and eventually have sex with.

How very different for a girl who feels sexually and emotionally drawn to girls rather than boys, or for a boy who is only interested in boys. How do these kids feel about themselves when they become aware of their different-ness at an age where everyone needs to be the same? How are they going to explain to their parents that they will never bring home a person of the opposite sex and introduce them as their partner? How many gay people live with their sexual orientation as a secret which they never disclose or live? With religious groups still bedevilling a perfectly normal sexual variation to the theme and homophobia rife amongst those who use any excuse to make a scapegoat of others, it is still hard to come out.

Affirmations
- I am who I am and I am proud of it.
- I fully accept and appreciate my sexuality.
- I have a right just like everyone else to live my sexuality joyfully with a loving partner.

Script
I love and accept my sexuality exactly the way it is. I live in peace and harmony with myself, I treat myself with respect and I move through this world with dignity. I am a beautiful person. I am strong and centred. My self-belief and confidence grow with each day. I am accepting of others and others accept me. I am unique, just like everyone else, and I am proud of my uniqueness as a human being. I have the ability to love and I am loveable. My love for myself and others carries me safely through my life and helps me find that special person who wants to share my love with me. I am dignified, I am centred and I am strong. I am who I am, and I am proud of it.

Tips and tricks

1. If you are not comfortable with your sexuality, or not entirely sure, you can get help from organisations like PACE (*see* Useful Addresses, pages 235–7) who offer counselling sessions and seminars for gay men and women.

2. Whether you come out or not, and when you come out is entirely your decision. It is worth remembering that life becomes less complicated once you are out because you don't have to pretend any more.

3. Coming out does not have to be in-your-face. Choose who you tell with care, especially at work, but be prepared that word will travel.

4. WALK TALL!

CHILDREN

Anyone who has children will know that they change your life irrevocably. It is a good idea to think carefully whether you want children or not, so that you are clear about your own wishes. Once you get into a loving and committed relationship, the same question needs to be discussed early on because it is essential that both partners want the same. For some people, having a family is their greatest happiness, for others, it is not the right thing. To allow yourself to become pregnant even though you know your partner does not want children is unfair, not only towards your partner but also towards the child.

Once the first child is there, you need to learn a whole new way of being. A baby is totally and utterly dependent on you. It needs you for everything all the time for a considerable period of time to come, and this requires great patience and a strong relationship between the parents. And this continues for the next eighteen years, if not longer . . .

In this section, we will be looking first of all at the problem of infertility in men and women and then at various issues arising in connection with children.

INFERTILITY

When you are emotionally ready to start a family, you may sometimes have to be patient. Having taken the contraceptive pill can draw out the process of becoming pregnant because your body needs to find its own natural hormonal balance again before you can conceive. Stress is another factor that can influence your ability to get pregnant.

When there is a true physical or biological reason why you don't get pregnant, either on your part or on that of your partner, medical advice and intervention might be the way forward. But, in the meantime, there is a lot you can do to give your body and mind the right balance to encourage conception.

Affirmations for the woman
- My body is relaxed and my mind is calm as I lovingly open myself to conception.
- Every fibre and every cell of my body is now balancing itself to receive the sperm and carry it towards fruition.
- I look forward to easy and effortless conception.

Affirmations for the man
- My body is becoming stronger and more powerful as I am lovingly releasing my sperm towards its aim.
- My sperm is increasing in volume and travels quickly forward.
- My body releases its semen efficiently and effectively towards its aim.

Script for the woman
I am calm and relaxed. All my senses are balanced and strong. My body is in perfect balance. My inner feelings of peace and tranquillity fill my body and mind. All the energies in my body are in perfect harmony; all the muscles, all the muscle

fibres and every single cell in my body are tuned into the frequency of successful conception. Every cell in my body vibrates to the frequency of successful conception. Conception is easy and I look forward to having a happy, healthy baby at the end of it. My body is in readiness, my mind is in readiness. I am centred and strong as I relax into successful conception.

Script for the man
I am calm and relaxed. All my senses are balanced and strong. My body is in perfect harmony. My inner feelings of strength and power fill my body and mind. All the energies in my body are in perfect harmony and are focussed on releasing my sperm efficiently and effectively towards its aim. All the energies in my body are in perfect balance; all the muscles and muscle fibres and every single cell in my body are tuned into the perfect frequency for fertilisation. My sperm increases in volume, my sperm travels fast and efficiently, it goes straight to its aim and successful fertilisation is a certainty.

Scenario for the woman
Imagine sperm travelling up the fallopian tube and a sperm implanting itself in an egg. Watch the fallopian passageway clear and imagine the sperm travelling quickly and in great numbers.

Scenario for the man
Imagine your sperm increasing in volume. Watch the sperm mobile, teeming with activity, moving vigorously. See in your mind's eye how your sperm moves forward energetically towards the fallopian tubes, pushing forward. Imagine lots of sperm reaching the egg, with one sperm settling in successfully.

Tips and tricks
1. Sex is for fun, not just for producing babies. Stop counting for the fertile days. Instead, make sex more enjoyable and interesting and do it *whenever*. You will get pregnant anyway.

2. Do the scenarios regularly every day, whether you will be having sex or not. They are particularly effective if you do them together with your partner, holding hands.

3. Eating the right foods will help fertility. Women who want to conceive need high intakes of zinc, magnesium, iron, essential fatty acids and vitamins A, C and E. For male fertility, vitamins A, B, C and E, zinc and selenium are essential. You can derive all of these vitamins and minerals from the foods you eat. Avocado, for example, is high in potassium, contains healthy mono-unsaturated oils and is a provider of vitamins A, B and E. Pumpkin and sesame seeds are rich in zinc and vitamin E. Dates, apricots, citrus fruit, dark-green vegetables, olives, carrots, oats, oily fish, cheese, free range poultry and lean lamb all provide good nutrition and a good range of vitamins, minerals and proteins.

4. *For men*: Research has shown that avoiding alcohol altogether raises the sperm count considerably and also raises sperm motility.

5. *For men*: Smoking is one of the commonest causes of damaged sperm. Smoking also destroys vitamin C, needed by sperm to function properly.

6. *For men*: Wear comfortable underwear. Tight clothing raises the body temperature around the testicles and this results in sperm cells becoming less active.

7. *For women*: Do not embark on a diet when you want to conceive. Cut down on exercise. Being too thin or doing too much exercise can stop you ovulating and menstruating.

Sandra and Oliver's Story
Sandra (30) and Oliver (27) had been trying for a baby for six months without success. They both had themselves checked out

by their doctor who could not find any reason why the couple should not conceive. Physically they were both fine. However, both of them held stressful positions at work and they often found that they were overwrought in the evenings and experienced difficulty in switching off.

It was Sandra who came to see me. She said she knew that her inability to relax had something to do with the problem. She was also concerned about the changes that a baby would bring to their lifestyle and about the consequences for her job and career. It was really Oliver who was keen on children – she felt ambiguous about a pregnancy although she had never really been aware of this herself until she came for her first session with me.

It turned out that her biggest problem was the thought of having to give up her career in order to look after the baby. 'There is no point in having a baby if you just go and hand it over to a childminder. I feel I would not be happy with myself if I did that,' Sandra explained. And yet, she could not see herself as a 'mumsy' woman who would stay at home and look after the baby.

Once she became aware of her reservations, she was able to look at solutions that would allow her to have a baby *and* keep her hand in with her job by working part-time from home. This helped her feel less stressed and soon afterwards, she became pregnant, much to her and Oliver's delight.

PARENTHOOD

Being a parent is a full-time job that, despite its high demands on your emotions and patience, can still be done by anyone without qualifications or training. It is a job that requires maturity, confidence and lots of love to make it rewarding and fun both for you and your children. If you have hang ups or fears, it is a good idea to make sure you get them sorted out before you have children, so that your children have a greater chance to grow up without similar fears.

Affirmations
- My child is my treasure and I love it immeasurably.
- I can learn to bring up my child with love and patience.
- I can learn to adapt to my children's needs while teaching them to adapt themselves to other people's needs.

Script

I commence my role as a parent with love and patience. I take pleasure in observing the development and the different personalities of my children and in helping them achieve their potential. I feel a wonderful feeling of peace and harmony flowing through my body and mind. My harmonious feelings have a beneficial effect on those around me, including my children. We have fun together and laugh a lot. Any problems are immediately talked through and sorted out, calmly and lovingly. I am creating an atmosphere of openness and warmth in my family. Everyone is entitled to their opinion. The needs of every family member are important, including my own. I take pleasure in my role as a parent. I am interested in my children and I follow their development with happiness and pride. There is a good atmosphere around us all, and our house is open to welcome our children's friends. I love to be with my children but I also accept and respect their need for privacy.

Scenario

Imagine yourself laughing and talking with your children, helping them and watching them develop.

Tips and tricks

1. Do read up on child rearing but don't overdo it. Pick whatever advice appeals to you and stick to it.

2. Each of your children is unique, with a particular blend of strengths and weaknesses. Your children's characteristics may be directly opposed to your own. This does not make your children automatically into losers. Make sure you do not try to foist your own dreams on to your children. If your child lacks the academic skills to become a lawyer, it can still achieve success and happiness as a carpenter. It is better to let go of your dreams for your child and help your child achieve its own dreams.

3. If your children are getting on your nerves, make sure you stop them in their tracks (*see also* Consistency, below). There are no prizes to be won for being too lenient.

4. Organise your month in such a way that you get an occasional evening off from the children. You can either take turns with babysitting by arranging a schedule with neighbours and friends who also have children, or you can get a babysitter every once in a while. Make sure you also spend some quality time with your partner. Happy parents have happy children.

5. Keep a flow of communication going between you and the children. Tell them about your life (but not about your problems), your childhood and your plans, and encourage them to talk about their achievements, concerns and worries. This way you create an atmosphere of openness in which it becomes easier to talk about problems.

6. Do not expect your children to display virtues that you yourself cannot muster. Teach by example. Honesty, reliability, warmth and openness have to come from you first before your children can develop these qualities themselves.

CONSISTENCY

Over the years there have been various schools of thought about how to bring up your children, from the Victorian 'children should be seen not heard' to the laissez-faire attitude of Summerhill School where children could decide what they wanted to learn.

But it is not so much what we *read* about child rearing that influences our decisions when it comes to bringing up our offspring, it is our own experiences as children that will have an effect on our performance as parents. Depending on our own childhood and personality type, one of three things normally happen:

- We go on doing exactly the same our parents did even though this made us unhappy as children. This is the 'It never did me any harm to be hit' school of thought.
- We make a determined effort to do things very differently from our parents because we remember how unhappy we were as children with the way our parents treated us.
- We continue in our parent's tradition because it worked for us as children.

Adults with the best chances of succeeding as parents are those in the last group because they are in a habit of being treated in an acceptable way and simply copy this behaviour. Parents in the middle category can also do very well. Their own unhappiness about certain problems they had with their parents has had such a deep effect on them that they make a special effort to avoid the same mistakes.

For people in the first group, progress is near impossible. A lack of consideration of their feelings and needs has led to them closing up to such an extent that they cannot get to their own feelings any more, let alone those of others. Professional help would be needed to enable them to see their own hurt and deal with it, but as long as the person lacks the insight of their own hurt, they will not seek help.

Apart from love, endless patience, a sense of fun and a positive attitude, one factor in bringing up children is vital: consistency. If you keep on making rules and breaking them or if you allow your children to disregard them, your children will lack the safety of a structure to support them. This does not mean that rules have to be adhered to come what may. There are occasional situations where an exception has to be made, and that is fine. However, on the whole, rules that have been agreed to need to be stuck to.

Affirmations
- I love my children and I give them a clear structure to support them.
- It is OK for me to be firm and consistent.
- I can be loving and consistent at the same time.

Script
My love and respect for my children govern all my actions. I recognise them for what they are: little individuals who need my help to unfold their potential as they grow and develop. They are carried forward in their life by my love and support. While they are still learning about themselves and the world around them, they need the clear structure that only a parent can give them. I recognise that I am helping channel their potential in a positive way by giving them the guidelines and gentle rules that govern successful human interaction. As I myself live those rules I teach them to my children. And when my children forget the rules, it is OK for me to remind them. I can be confident and persistent in a loving way. My consistency helps my children feel safe and secure. My consistency gives them a chance of getting things right.

Scenario
Imagine a recent event where you were inconsistent with your child/children. Replay the scene in your mind, but this time imagine yourself being consistent and following through what you asked for.

Tips and tricks
1. Consistency helps children to stick to given rules better. Frequent inconsistency invalidates rules and makes children insecure or manipulative.

2. Make sure you lead by example. Do not ask of your children what you are unwilling or unable to do yourself.

3. Consistency has nothing to do with shouting, it has to do with calmly sticking to your guns.

4. If you make a rule, it needs to be made public to the entire family. When a rule is made, it should also be discussed what are the consequences of not following the rule. For example, if your fourteen-year-old is allowed out until 10 p.m. at the weekend but come home later, then they have to go without their mobile phone for three days.

5. Once rules have been established, they can be broken occasionally, but only for a good reason and not just on a whim.

6. The same rules have to apply to all your children, unless it is an age-specific rule. Older children should have more freedom than younger children. However, helping clear the dishes or wash up needs to involve *all* of them, including handicapped children to the best of their ability.

7. At times, in fact *most* of the time, your children will feel hassled by having to stick to the rules. This is unavoidable and does not necessarily mean the rules are wrong, so don't be swayed!

Joanne's Story
Joanne (33) was at the end of her tether. Her thirteen-year-old daughter Daisy would not do her homework. She was, Joanne felt, a perfectly intelligent child with a lot of potential but she had all sorts of excuses when it came to doing any work for school. She spent hours on the phone to her friends and listening to her CDs, and then she claimed that she was too tired to do homework. Daisy's favourite sentence was, 'Don't hassle me. I'll do it in a minute.' But that famous minute did not often occur.

After a positive thinking session, Joanne understood that she needed to make clearer rules and stick to them. She explained to Daisy that she needed to do her homework regularly in order to be successful at school. Joanne also explained that she *expected* Daisy to do her homework every day. She designated the dining table as 'homework table' as there were fewer distractions there than in Daisy's room. If Daisy did not do her homework she would not be allowed to use the phone to ring her friends. Joanne also insisted on seeing the homework Daisy had done once she had finished it.

Joanne stuck to this rule consistently and was surprised and delighted how well it worked. Daisy's performance in school improved considerably and Joanne felt less stressed by the homework situation.

SCHOOL PHOBIA

A school phobia is a serious problem and has nothing to do with the listlessness most kids display at having to get up early. When a previously happy child begins to develop a fear of going to school, it can be for a number of reasons. If your child is particularly sensitive and has just changed schools, there may be initial nerves about the new kids and environment. This anxiety will slowly abate as your child gets used to the new school. However, when your child has been going to the school for a while and begins to be more anxious about going, look out for any of the following reasons:

- bullying
- overly strict teacher/s
- fear of failure (are you putting too much pressure on your child to succeed?)
- fear of failure (is the school putting too much pressure on your child to succeed?)
- an oppressive workload
- dyslexia
- problems at home

The only way you will find out is to speak to your child and also to the teacher or teachers. Children are often ashamed of admitting that they are bullied or they may not want to admit that they can't cope and therefore may deny it.

Just like in the chapter on divorce, you can help your child by doing the school phobia affirmations and script with the child or, if they are old enough, let them do the exercises by themselves. Please remember that with any fear, it is important to use the Relaxation Script (*see* page 90) first before going on to the phobia script.

Affirmations
- I can learn to stay calm and relaxed when I go to school.
- My confidence is getting stronger and every day it is becoming easier to go to school.
- Things are beginning to sort themselves out and I can become stronger.

Script
Very soon I am beginning to get calmer and more relaxed. I can learn to become more confident and tackle the problems to do with school in a more relaxed way. I am on my way to finding solutions to my problems and I can find someone else to help me. Slowly, my problems begin to disappear and with every day I feel happier being me. Things start getting easier and I am beginning to feel more confident about going to school. My performance at school improves and I begin to achieve things much more easily. I speak more easily to the other kids and I can speak up whenever I need to. Everyone is amazed at the progress I am making and soon I find it hard to understand why I was ever worried about school.

Scenario
You have an imaginary friend who helps you in tricky situations. Your friend is big and strong and is always by your side, giving you confidence and encouraging you at school.

Tips and tricks

1. Don't carry around your problems all by yourself. If you are having problems at school or at home, try and find an adult to talk to about them.

2. If the other pupils or the teachers at your school frighten you with their behaviour, it may be better for you to change schools. When you are afraid a lot of the time, you cannot learn properly.

3. If you find reading and writing difficult, tell your parents about it. An educational kinesiologist will be able to help you read and write much better so your schoolwork improves. (Educational kinesiology is chiefly used for improving learning skills. As with Health Kinesiology, it uses muscle testing to identify stresses and imbalances that are caused by certain activities and movements affecting co-ordination and performance in many learning situations. Imbalances can be caused by eye movements and head positions such as looking down which can impair a child's ability to read.)

4. If a particular teacher is always picking on you, talk to your parents about it. They can speak to the teacher to find out what the problem is.

Ben's Story

Ben (8) had developed a very strong school phobia over the last year. His father Roger brought him to me to see whether something could be achieved with hypnotherapy. On speaking to both of them in detail, I noticed how the father kept interrupting his son and generally being very domineering. He was impatient for his son to 'get a grip' and 'pull himself together' and asked me if I could assist.

It appeared to me that part of Ben's problem was his overbearing father, so I invited the father back for a second time on his own. I explained to him that it might be beneficial for him to come in for a few sessions to learn how to handle his son better so that he would be willing to go back to school again. In his sessions, it turned out that Roger had been bullied by his parents and had been very unhappy as a child. Once Roger had worked through these issues, his attitude to Ben changed and Ben went to school happily once again.

STEPCHILDREN

Though divorce rates are high, second marriages are not uncommon, with the result that two families have to merge. If it is a challenge to bring up your own children, it is even more challenging to bring up your own *and* someone else's. Problems can occur on different levels:

- you don't get on with your partner's children
- your partner's children don't get on with you
- your children don't get on with your partner's children or vice versa
- you disagree with your partner about his/her treatment of his/her children
- you disagree with your partner about his/her treatment of your children
- your partner doesn't get on with your children
- your children don't get on with your partner

It takes bundles of tolerance, understanding, love and patience to make this new family merger work.

Affirmations
- I can learn to live with my new children in peace and harmony.
- My feelings of love expand and extend to encompass my entire new family.
- I allow myself the time to get to know my new family. I am calmly interested.

Script

I have the strength and wisdom to act with love as I am integrating the new children into my family. We are gently and gradually drawing closer to one another as we are beginning to learn about each other. I appreciate the differences my new children bring into my life. I can adjust and readjust for them, just as I can help them adjust and readjust to me and my children. I am leading gently and firmly, I am impartial and just. I stay calm and relaxed. I observe closely and act lovingly but firmly. My new partner and I work together in harmony and with mutual respect. The bond with my partner strengthens as we make united decisions concerning our children. All our children become integrated. They are bonded to me and my partner with love. Together we are strong.

Scenario

Imagine having a meal together with the entire new family, with everybody happily chatting, then clearing the table together.

Tips and tricks

1. If you have no children but your partner does, assume the role of maternal/paternal friend to the children but leave the actual responsibilities to your partner. Assure your partner that they are the best possible mother/father their child could have, even if you don't agree with their methods. Let them get on with the job. If your partner is too indulgent with their children, they will need to take the rap later on if things go wrong. Be there for the children as a friend they can talk to or even complain to, but if any decisions have to be made, refer them back to their mother/father. The more you keep out of it, the less stress will be put on your relationship with your partner and the more harmonious family life can be.

2. If both you and your partner bring children into the relationship, it is vital that any rules that are made are adhered to by *all* the children. Impartiality must be preserved at all cost.

3. As parents you need to present a united front to the children. Discuss differences in opinion in private, then announce your consensus to all the children. When your children are old enough, you can have a family meeting around the table where problems are aired and resolved together.

Sonja's Story

Sonja (45) met Anthony after having been single for a year after her divorce. They were well-suited and fell in love quickly, feeling they had found the right partner. They both wanted to stay together. Sonja did not have children, Anthony had two teenage daughters of thirteen and fifteen who had lived with him since his divorce six months earlier. They all got on very well together, although Sonja felt that the girls were quite spoilt and Anthony too lenient. When the younger stepdaughter started becoming unruly and hanging out with the wrong kind of friends, Sonja knew the answer – Anthony had to be stricter. Anthony saw Sonja's point but found it difficult to be consistent. This annoyed Sonja and it began to negatively influence her relationship with her younger stepdaughter.

In a session, she found out that she felt angry at the stepdaughter's bad behaviour but, in reality, she was angry at her partner for not taking more control of the situation. Sonja agreed to a trial period of two weeks during which she would let Anthony get on with dealing with the situation in his own way. Sonja was allowed to listen to his problems sympathetically (if possible), but not give any advice or opinion.

As a result, Anthony sorted things out his own way and this allowed his relationship with Sonja to stay intact. When further problems with the younger stepdaughter occurred, Sonja again left it to Anthony to sort things out. Slowly, Anthony began to see for himself that he needed to make clearer rules and stick to them if he wanted things to work out better between his daughter and himself. He had needed to find his feet as a father because, in the past, his ex-wife had been the disciplinarian for the girls. Sonja was happy that Anthony had become more consistent and Anthony felt supported by Sonja in a positive way.

CHAPTER SIX

Work Life

O ur working environment and the *way* we work has changed beyond all recognition since the late 1980s. With the mass use of computers and other communication equipment we have become much more independent of location. It does not matter if we don't go to the office today – so long as we have a computer link at home or wherever else we are, we can still do our work. In teleconferences, a host of people from different countries can speak to one another as if they were meeting in the same room. Not only is such a meeting cheap to arrange, but it also makes it so much easier to convene. Modern technology saves businesses time and money and many of the changes it brings are really wonderful.

New technology has created new opportunities, and these are now increasingly seized by the younger sections of society. Over the last ten years or so, there has been a trend of children moving straight from school into business. Instead of going into further education, they set up on their own straight away, sometimes while they are still at school. All that is needed is a viable idea and a computer. Some sixty per cent of UK households have a computer today, and lots of people have creative ideas. Some of the wealthiest people have gone from school straight into business, something which was unheard of only twenty years ago. Think about it: if you order something via the Internet you don't really know who is on the other end. For all you know, it could be an eighteen-year-old running his own business from his bedroom.

With technology moving fast, new products move into the marketplace quickly, but the competition also copies your ideas faster! As a consequence, you have to come up with new ideas more often, change your advertising more often and think of new incentives for customers to buy your product. As an employee, the fierce competition may result in you getting laid off or having new tasks assigned to you that were not in your original job description. Rather than looking for a new job, you may want to, or feel you *have* to, tackle these new challenges head on and learn the appropriate skills. However, learning new skills while still working to earn a living can be stressful, and not everyone feels confident they can take on board and assimilate new information, particularly when the last time they had to study was when they went to school. But if you want to progress in your job, and especially when you want to move up the career ladder, you are expected to be informed and on top of the latest developments in your field. When you are already feeling stressed or when you are having problems with learning, it can be difficult to retain new information and this can seriously thwart your efforts of progressing in your career.

Other changes which require a lot of adaptability are becoming self-employed, or going from working from a place outside your home to working from home. This can bring the problems of isolation and a lack of a given work structure. It requires a lot of self-motivation and perseverance to make working from home a success.

But even when you are employed and working for a company, sharing your work environment with others, you need to be able to adapt. Wherever people get together, there is potential conflict. When you join an existing group of workers, they will have their own particular idiosyncrasies and methods of working which may clash with your own, and this can lead to problems within the work group. Being able to get on with work colleagues is very important. The necessary social skills that make you a good colleague in a work environment should have been acquired throughout your younger years during your time at school. If you find that social interaction is not your strong point, you need to learn this skill now! Without being a good team player, you won't achieve your full potential and you won't enjoy your time at work. Considering that we spend a large proportion of our waking hours at work, this would be a great shame.

FLEXIBILITY

What is required today as a basic skill in your work life is flexibility and this is why flexibility is the key theme for this chapter. As long as you can adapt in a relaxed way by adopting an optimistic attitude, you will be able to deal with changes in your work environment in a productive and effective way, allowing you to keep stress levels to a minimum. We also need flexibility to learn and develop within our career. If you can be flexible, you can stay calmer in the face of the changes around you, and that puts you at an advantage.

Affirmations
- I adapt easily to changes and make the best of every situation.
- I am flexible, calm and strong. My flexibility gives me an advantage.
- My flexibility allows me to turn challenging situations into amazing opportunities.

Script
As life around me changes, I stay calm and positive. I observe attentively what is happening while my mind registers in detail the changes around me. I relax while I am allowing my subconscious mind to process my observations. My subconscious mind is always working for me night and day to come up with solutions and answers to any life situation. As I am beginning to rely on my intuition, I am pleased and delighted how ingeniously my mind assists me in finding alternatives and clarifications. I am discovering how easily I can adapt to new situations that

work life brings. I am flexible and strong, and my subconscious mind is always there to help me. I feel pleasantly detached from problems. As my subconscious mind deals with them, I can stay calm and relaxed. I regard problems as stepping stones to a better future. My optimism is unshakable. I am flexible and strong and always ride on top of the waves of life. I stay positive, whatever comes. I find constructive solutions that are positive for me and everyone else around me.

Scenario
Imagine yourself like a cork on the ocean. No matter how high the waves get, the cork always floats on top. Imagine feeling safe and secure, because you are unsinkable.

Tips and tricks
1. When things around you are changing and you feel these changes are outside your control, take the attitude that this is the best thing that could have happened to you. It is easy to feel resentful, hurt or stressed when life forces changes upon you, but it is much more constructive to pretend that these changes are to your advantage. Invariably, your positive attitude will see to it that the changes work out for the best.

2. When you feel you need to make changes within your working life, make sure you consult with your family. Any changes you make will affect them as well, and it is important that everyone is heard. This does not mean that you should let your family run your career, but knowing what unsettles your partner or your children about the proposed changes will allow everyone to think about solutions that take into account everyone's needs.

3. Be aware that flexibility is a life skill that will stand you in good stead, not only in your work environment but also in other life situations. The world is moving fast these days, and if you are flexible you can enjoy the ride, rather than want to get off because of the stress the changes cause you.

Once you have a handle on flexibility, the problems you face in the workplace can be easier to deal with. Following are strategies for dealing with some of the most common problems we face today.

WORK PROBLEMS AND SOLUTIONS

ASSERTIVENESS

Ideally, you will have learnt in childhood how to interact successfully with other people in a group. Working well in a team is crucial in order to tackle a work project and bring it to a successful conclusion. One of the skills of a good employer is to choose their employees carefully and then create a working climate where there is good communication from the top down and from the bottom up. When employees feel they are taken seriously, that they are considered important and that their concerns are taken into account, they work better, take less days off sick and stay loyal to their employer.

In many companies, the situation is less than ideal, with employees bringing their own personal baggage with them into their work, which they then inflict on their colleagues. Still, you can't just walk out of a job because you don't like the atmosphere. The mortgage and bills still have to be paid. However, if the problem lies with you, there is a lot you can do to increase your confidence levels so that you can enjoy your time at work more, work better and more efficiently, and derive greater satisfaction out of your job.

CONFIDENCE IN GROUPS

For many employees, a lack of confidence when in meetings is a problem. Everyone is sitting around a table to discuss a project and you are part of that group but dare not speak up. You may have valuable points to contribute but your heart starts racing, your mouth dries up and you can't get a word out. If someone addresses you, you stammer and things come out in a garbled fashion. You feel embarrassed about the unprofessional delivery of your opinion, you criticise yourself for your failure to speak clearly and succinctly and you become even more afraid of the next meeting.

Affirmations

- I am well prepared and I have something important to contribute.
- I can learn to say what I have to say calmly and confidently.
- People in the meeting want to hear what I have to say. My contribution is valuable.

Script

I am a valuable member of the team. My contributions to the project are important and my opinions count. I have a right to demand respect for any contributions, and I demand this respect from others as well as from myself. Out of respect for my own contribution to the project I speak up. My breathing is easy and regular, my movements are natural and free. I am taking myself seriously from now on. My opinion may be right or wrong, but it needs to be heard. I am speaking calmly and easily, I am speaking slowly and deliberately. This is about the project, not me. No matter whether I am right or wrong, my contribution needs to be heard. Even when another opinion is preferred over mine, that is OK. This is about the project, not me. We are all in the same boat. Everyone is contributing to the best of their ability to make this project a success. I am one of the team. I count and my opinion is valuable.

Scenario
Imagine yourself in a meeting, breathing easily, speaking freely. Imagine others responding positively to what you are saying.

Tips and tricks
1. Always do a Relaxation Script first (*see* page 90) before you use your script or scenario.

2. Make an achievement ladder for improved confidence in meetings. It could look like this:

- **Scenario 1** – agreeing with someone else verbally in the meeting (not just nodding!)
- **Scenario 2** – asking a question in the meeting
- **Scenario 3** – making a short comment about something someone else has said
- **Scenario 4** – saying a few sentences which express some facts you know about
- **Scenario 5** – giving your opinion on something (which may not be substantiated by facts but merely an opinion)

You then do your Relaxation Script first, followed by the visualisation of Scenario 1. You practise this mentally for at least three days, then try it out in reality. Once you have acted out Scenario 1 in a real-life meeting, go on to visualising Scenario 2 and then test it in reality. Continue until you have done all five steps of your achievement ladder in reality.

3. Help your body cope with your nerves by taking ten Tissue Salt No. 6 tablets twice a day while you are going through the learning process.

FEAR OF AUTHORITY

Some people are fine with colleagues and in meetings, but fearful and overawed by anyone who is in a higher position than them. Whereas they are normally quite eloquent, they become shy, embarrassed, flustered or tongue-tied when faced with someone in authority. This is often the case even when the superior is friendly and accessible.

The reason for this fear is often to be found in negative childhood experiences, either at home or at school. In other cases, it is just a very low level of self-esteem that causes the anxiety.

Affirmations

- I can learn to be calm and professional in the presence of people in authority.
- I can learn to be myself in the presence of princes and paupers alike.
- The great are only great because I am on my knees.

Script

I am now beginning to build my confidence and self-esteem. Day by day, I am feeling more in tune with myself. I am aware of my value as a human being and I have decided to stop being judgemental about people in authority. I give everyone a fair chance to prove that they are professional and reasonable, no matter whether they work above or below me. I am being fair and reasonable myself and disregard status. As my confidence grows, I am becoming more calm and more relaxed. I treat everyone the same, no matter what their position. I am calm and relaxed. I am polite and professional. I feel comfortable with my new non-judgemental attitude.

Scenario

Picture yourself in comfortable conversation with your superior, listening attentively and responding freely.

Tips and tricks

1. Think about where you learnt in the past that people in authority are frightening. Was it a teacher? A relative? Someone in church? If you remember someone who has instilled that fear in you, close your eyes and imagine that person standing in front of you. If you feel they were a good person but mismanaged the situation with you, imagine handing them back the fear they have given you. It does not belong to you. It was never yours in the first place.

2. If you feel the person who instilled the fear in you was malicious, you can also do the following:

- Close your eyes and remember what happened with that person in the past.
- Put the old memory on to an inner screen in your mind and watch the memory as an adult outside observer.
- When you see the person in authority threatening or frightening the screen-You, you can go into the screen as an adult outside observer and tell off the person in authority in no uncertain terms. If you feel like it, imagine yelling at them or beating them up if you feel their conduct deserves it. Let off steam in your mind. It's only in your imagination and quite safe.

3. Remember that there is no obligation on your part to continue feeling scared of people in authority. You can decide that from now on, they get classified as fallible human beings together with everyone else.

Peter's Story

Peter (52) was generally a confident person but when it came to work meetings, he lost his nerve. He was foreman in a factory, and whenever the big bosses wanted a meeting, they invited Peter to attend. Peter tried to get out of attending by making excuses or hiding behind his workload, but when a meeting was rescheduled to make sure he could attend, Peter could no longer avoid showing his face. 'It's not the bosses as such,' he said, 'they are all right. It is more their position that scares me to death.'

With Peter, I first had to do some exploratory work to find out where he had learnt to believe that figures of authority had to be feared. In two sessions of analytical hypnotherapy, Peter worked through some memories of his schooldays with brethren, some of whom had a cruel streak. They had beaten the boys and threatened them with hellfire and damnation unless they toed the line.

Once the reason for his fears had been worked through, Peter found it a lot easier to go through the scenario of speaking confidently with his bosses, and the very next week he was able to do so in reality.

INTELLECTUAL SKILLS

With the pace of technological change and new developments in products and services, there is a need today to keep up with future trends. This might entail going on courses or studying professional journals at home after work. Equally, when you are just starting a new job, you may be required to learn new information in order to do your job well.

Your school days may be a long time behind you when you find you need to retrain or to beef up on advanced knowledge in your professional field. You may no longer be used to sitting over books and articles, taking notes or committing new information to memory. Worse still, if you never acquired learning skills at all because you left school early or were never taught a structure to help you learn efficiently, studying can be very hard.

LEARNING NEW THINGS

Learning something new, be it a practical skill or acquiring more theoretical knowledge, can be great fun. If you had a bad time at school, try and leave it behind you as best you can. With the right instructions and a positive approach, learning can be a rewarding process that builds your confidence and gives you a better chance to climb the career ladder.

In the following affirmations, script and scenario, I have picked a situation where you study from books. This makes the following suggestions suitable for adults in paid employment or studying for higher qualifications as well as university and secondary school students.

Affirmations
– Learning is easy and it is fun to find out new information that helps me progress.
– With every day I am enjoying studying more.
– I look forward to achieving good results as I get happily involved in learning new things.

Script
I am making a fresh start and I have decided that, from today on, learning new things is fun. I concentrate on what I am reading, I am calm and relaxed and focussed on the text. I read each paragraph until I understand it and then move on. I take in new information easily and effortlessly and I take pride in preparing my work well for my next assignment/the next school day. I take notes where appropriate, and the more I read the more I get involved in the process of learning. Time goes quickly as I concentrate fully on the text in front of me. My involvement in my work makes it more and more interesting to study, and as my knowledge increases, so does my confidence and my sense of purpose.

Scenario
Imagine yourself having acquired all the necessary knowledge and see yourself reaping the benefits/passing your exams or working in a much better position thanks to your additional qualifications.

Tips and tricks

1. While you are studying, turn off any sources of distraction such as the radio or television. Even if you are used to studying while having music on, try a few days without. It is amazing how much background sounds can divert your attention from studying, especially when there are words sung or spoken with the music. Instrumental music, faintly in the background, tends to be OK.

2. Take your time when you are studying. It is better to learn less and to learn it thoroughly than to study a great deal of material and only do so superficially. Continue with the course material *only* when you have fully understood what you have studied so far. In case of doubt, ring a schoolfriend or a tutor to clarify those matters that are unclear.

3. Keep your desk tidy. Have everything that you need to study ready and lined up. Turn the answering machine on and the telephone off. And leave the fridge alone! Concentrate on studying only. Breaks are fine, but don't wander off too far.

4. Drink water, hot or cold, as it helps the nerves fire better and this makes learning easier.

5. Divide your study time into manageable sections and give yourself a little reward at the end of each section. Get up and stretch your legs or go and get yourself a drink. Breaks of five to ten minutes are helpful as they allow the last lot of studying to sink in.

Thelma's Story

Thelma (49) was in the lucky position of having retained her job when several of her colleagues had been made redundant in a merger operation. What worried her was the fact that the new management had made it clear to her that she was expected to upgrade her IT skills. Even though Thelma had been using computers to a limited extent, she did not feel very confident at the thought of 'going back to school' as she called it. Her childhood experiences had not been pleasant when it came to learning new things, and she felt very apprehensive. 'If I didn't have to do it to keep my job, I would avoid it,' she confessed.

First of all Thelma had to learn how to relax physically and mentally. She did this by using the Relaxation Script (*see* page 90) and the correct breathing exercise (*see* page 30). We then put affirmations and a script together for her, similar to the ones you find in this chapter. For Thelma, it was important to add the sentence 'I have learnt things in the past, I can learn things in the future' to her script, and she also used this sentence as one of her affirmations. Thelma realised that she must have an in-built ability to learn since she had taught herself the basics of the word-processing package on her computer. Thelma used her script and affirmations three times every day by reading them five times in a row. After only a week, her confidence had increased enough for her to start looking forward to her IT course.

MEMORY

One of the greatest handicaps when you are trying to learn a new thing is poor memory. You can put in hours of work only to find that at the end of it you have retained little or nothing. This is discouraging and undermines any motivation you might have to study.

There are several reasons for bad memory:

- **Insufficient attention to what is being studied** – When you are not concentrating on what you are doing, you will retain the information less well or not at all. Concentration is the main factor in developing a good memory.
- **Incomplete understanding of course material** – You may think that you have understood what you have read, but sometimes it is easy to confuse two things:

you either merely follow the train of thought of the text you are reading, or you make a mental picture of the contents of what you have just read. Only when you connect the new information with other knowledge you already have can you really say that you have truly understood what you have been studying.

- **Trying to take in too much** – There is a limit to the attention span of the human mind. If you overload it, only a few things will go in and therefore only a few things will be retrievable.
- **Not going over learnt material often enough** – Most of us have to spend time revising what we have learnt in order to commit knowledge to long-term memory. There are some simple guidelines for revision which you will find under 'Tips and tricks'.

Affirmations

- I can learn to improve my ability to retain information easily and effortlessly.
- My memory works well and I remember new information easily.
- My memory is improving with every day and I enjoy exercising it daily.

Script

My memory is a muscle that needs training. I am now beginning to exercise my memory muscle on a daily basis, and with every day, my memory improves a little bit more. I concentrate on what I am reading and I concentrate on what I am hearing. As I stay calm and relaxed while paying close attention to what I need to commit to memory, I find that anything I learn is being stored in a systematic way in my subconscious mind. Every piece of information that is of importance is tidily stowed away in my subconscious memory bank so that it is available at any time, easily and effortlessly. Whenever I need to access subconscious information, it is readily available and easily retrievable. Any information I need springs to mind effortlessly. I am pleased with the reliability of my memory.

Scenario

Imagine your subconscious memory bank as a well-ordered library inside your head where all the information you have acquired is stored in books, on videos and on tapes. Whenever you need to access the information, you simply reach for the relevant book, video or tape and read, watch or listen to what you need to recall.

Tips and tricks

1. You cannot remember something you have not understood. If you are unclear about something you are trying to learn, ask someone who can explain it to you. If you have not understood the matter entirely, you will not be able to make sense of it, and this prevents you from remembering it.

2. Help your memory-muscle to strengthen by doing little memory exercises. Look at an everyday object, for example your mobile phone or your watch, and really concentrate on all the details. Now close your eyes and try and recall as many of the details as possible. Then open your eyes and check whether you remembered everything.

3. If you find it difficult to remember written material, pick a small article in a paper or magazine and read it slowly and carefully. Put the paper away and repeat out loud what the article said, as if you had to summarise its contents for a friend. Check whether you got it right.

4. If is often helpful to make a mental picture of what you need to learn. Your memory is like a six-year-old – it likes cartoons! If you try to remember, for example, that veins carry blood *to* the heart and arteries carry blood *away* from the heart, you could picture blue lorries (= veins with blood that looks blue) driving towards a petrol pump (= the heart) and red sports cars (= arteries with blood that looks red) driving away from it.

5. Learn in small sections if you find it hard to concentrate, but keep at it. Go over a small section several times rather than try and do three sections without really taking it all in. Once your concentration improves, you can do more.

6. In order to store information in your long-term memory, you have to go over it several times. Repeat what you have learnt three times during the learning stint, once at the end of your learning session and then once again within the next twenty-four hours. Repeat it again in three days time. This will ensure that the information is stored firmly in your subconscious.

STRESS

No matter whether you look after children at home, run a household or go out to work every day, stress is a constant possibility. Typical examples of stressful situations are those where you have to perform or where there is a clash of interests in the work environment. But even pleasant events such as a promotion can create a feeling of anxiety.

GOING FOR INTERVIEWS

With many people applying for one advertised job, companies are in the position of being able to pick and choose. Where once few or no qualifications were needed for modest positions, standards have been raised by many companies who want to see at least some GCSE qualifications from applicants.

A second prerequisite to be successful in your application is that you present well during the interview, and this is where some struggle. It is a great shame when you are well qualified for a job but your nerves let you down so that you do not come across as well as you could during the interview and so you are unable to secure the position.

Affirmations
- I know my worth and I can come across as confident and professional.
- I look forward to a successful interview.
- I enjoy talking about my skills and my achievements in a calm and professional manner.

Script
I know my strengths and I am aware of my potential. I have prepared myself well for this interview and I look forward to meeting the new company. I am calm and collected, my breathing is steady and regular, my movements are light and free as I speak in a relaxed manner. I find it easy to answer any questions and I speak confidently about my past work experience. I enjoy the interview situation. My breathing is comfortable; my movements are free. I speak effortlessly about my strengths, my skills and my achievements. I feel free to ask questions myself and listen carefully to the answers that I am given. It is important to me to establish whether this position suits me. I know what I am worth, I have clear ideas about what I am looking for in a new job, and no matter how many interviews I attend, I remain calm and collected. I know I am coming across well. I find it easy to make a good impression.

Scenario
Imagine yourself well turned out and in an excellent mood as you go for your interview. See yourself move freely, hear yourself speak easily and effortlessly and imagine yourself answering any questions with ease.

Tips and tricks
1. Prepare well for your interview. Be clear about the skills

you can offer your potential new employer. You need to know which of your skills make you the right candidate for the job, so the more you find out about the job before and during the interview, the more easily you can emphasise those of your skills that fit the job.

2. Practise speaking out loud about your previous work experience so you can give a reasonably fluent account. Practise once a day for at least three days *before* the interview. On the day of the interview, *do not practise*; just relax by doing the Relaxation Script (*see* page 90) followed by your interview script.

3. Be aware that it is not just you who is being assessed during the interview but also the new company. It is unnecessary to be overawed just because you have been invited for an interview! Make sure that you consider carefully whether the new employer is good enough for you rather than constantly obsessing whether you are good enough for them.

4. What is it you want to know about your potential new employer? Make sure you clarify any questions you may have. If the post turns out to be different from what you expected or is altogether unsuitable, you may need to change jobs again shortly and that would not look good on your CV . . .

5. If you do not possess a skill that is required for the job but you feel you could acquire it, say so during the interview. Do *not* pretend you can do something you cannot do unless you are absolutely sure that you can pick up the necessary knowledge very quickly and easily.

6. If you feel that you did not get on well during the interview, check whether the interviewer had a way about him/her that made you nervous or confused. Don't feel it is necessarily only your fault!

Clare's Story

Clare (23) was the most nervous person I have ever seen at my practice. She found it nearly impossible to sit still. She fidgeted constantly while she reported that she was a bundle of nerves just *thinking* about a job interview she had been invited to in three weeks' time.

First of all, I persuaded her to sit back from the edge of her chair where she had been balancing since the start of our conversation. I then introduced her to the Relaxation Script (*see* page 90) and the correct breathing exercise (*see* page 30) to help her calm down generally. She was surprised at how quietly she could sit after these exercises. I sent her home with a tape recording of the exercises and asked her to listen to the tape every day until her next session.

In the following week, we started with the same relaxation script and then added a scenario of her interview. As Clare started to get nervous at the mere thought of an interview, I suggested she saw a screen in front of her inner eye. On this screen she could watch another young woman go for an interview and get through it successfully and calmly. This, Clare found easy to do as she was convinced that everyone found interviews easy except her! As the next step, Clare was to continue imagining that she could see a screen in front of her, but this time, the young woman in the screen was Clare herself. While Clare stayed the outside observer, she watched the film in which the screen-Clare mastered the interview situation calmly and with great professionalism. Clare felt quite comfortable with this visualisation and went away to practise this at home.

When Clare came back for her last session, she reported that she already felt a bit more confident about the interview. In the session, Clare practised going into the screen and being in the film, feeling confident and relaxed whilst going through the interview situation. She practised this last scene, together with her relaxation, every day before the interview. She rang me later to say that she had got on well with the real-life interview and felt she had presented herself favourably.

COMPETITIVENESS

In some firms, there is an unpleasant atmosphere of competition, making it stressful to work there. While some individuals like the idea of out-performing their colleagues, others experience this as a threat, putting them under constant pressure.

Competitiveness can be invigorating and fun as long as it stays free from intrigue and backstabbing. If the latter is the case, I would urgently recommend you reconsider whether you want to continue working for that company. An atmosphere of mistrust, criticism and lack of co-operation makes staff ill. Even though company politics are quite common, they do not exist everywhere. Considering you have to spend a great proportion of your waking hours at work, you should make sure you are happy there.

It is fine to strive for optimum performance, and it is OK to want to excel in what you are doing. It is *not* OK to hold it over others that you are doing better than them. If you feel uncomfortable with the competitive atmosphere in your office and you cannot leave your job at the moment, protect yourself with the following.

Affirmations
- I can stay dignified and calm as I move around in any work environment.
- My values and integrity remain intact, no matter who is around me.
- I only partake in positive and constructive actions when at work.

Script
I keep my sense of proportion and I hold on to what is important to me. I am safe and comfortable within myself. I feel comfortable striving for the best I can achieve in my job. I acknowledge my own achievements as much as I acknowledge

the achievements of others. Other than that, I am determined to participate in positive gossip only. Whatever anyone wishes to think about me is fine. Whatever anyone wishes to say about me is fine. It has no bearing on my positive frame of mind. My values stand firm, my confidence remains intact, no matter what is going on around me. Other people make their choices, I make mine. I have decided to behave with dignity and professionalism, and any negativity from others bounces off me. It is as if I had a protective shield around me, preventing anything untoward from touching me.

Scenario
Imagine you had a shield of white light around you that engulfs you from the soles of your feet to the top of your head. Imagine negativity from others bouncing off your shield and reflecting back to the sender.

Tips and tricks
1. If competitiveness in your work environment is really bad, do everything you can to change jobs. You will not change things for the better for yourself by remaining where you are, unless you are the boss. Your physical and mental health is at risk through the bad atmosphere. You can easily become ill or lose your confidence if you stay.

2. Keep out of company politics. You may feel tempted to comment on things that are going on – don't! If you participate in company politics you are helping to keep it going. The smaller the number of people who participate, the better the atmosphere. You will *not* be more popular if you take part in gossip.

3. Make sure the standard of your work is high so that others cannot attack you on a professional level.

DECISION-MAKING

If you avoid making decisions on a regular basis, you will end up not getting what you want. Apart from that, you are also likely to irritate others with your dithering . . .

Affirmations

- From today, I take responsibility for my own life and make my own decisions.
- I am willing and able to learn to make clear decisions.
- I now make up my mind once and for all, no matter what the consequences.

Script

I am now taking responsibility for my own life. Nobody can live my life for me and that is why I'm the best person to decide on the course of my life, be it right or wrong. No matter what happens, my decision stands. Once I have decided, I do everything in my power to make my decision work. With every day, I am becoming more competent at making the right decisions. I am happy and content being in charge of my own destiny. I am taking every decision after careful consideration of all the factors involved, and then I simply go ahead. I am beginning to understand better how to make the best possible choices, and my decisiveness is good for me and for all those around me. Even wrong decisions are helpful as I can learn from them and use them as springboards to better decisions. I make decisions easily.

Scenario

Imagine seeing two choices in front of your inner eye, for example 'further education' versus 'earning money'. As you are looking at each word in your mind, one of them will be more clearly outlined. Go for the option that looks clearer.

Tips and tricks

1. If you need to make a decision about a practical matter, make sure you gather all the information you can about the options available.

2. If you need to decide on a purely personal matter, check which option *feels* better. Should you get married to your current boyfriend or not? Close your eyes and imagine being married to him. While imagining this, *check what your body feels like.* If you notice unpleasant sensations in your stomach, heart area or in your head, he is not the one! If you get only neutral body sensations, he is not the one either! Only if your heart is 'jumping' with joy should you say 'yes'.

3. Some decisions you have to make will involve a number of other people. Don't carry the burden of decision-making all by yourself. Speak to everyone who will be affected by your decision. Ideally, get everyone together to discuss matters and to find the solution best for everyone.

4. Compromise is OK and sometimes the best option. It is not a sign of failure if you decide to compromise.

5. Remember that life is the unknown variable in your decision-making process. What seemed to be a sensible choice at the time can turn out to be a disaster. On the other hand, what seemed a crazy idea at first can work like a dream because circumstances change and things work out to your advantage.

PROMOTION

Attaining that better position is a happy event, but it can also lead to anxiety. A higher salary will go hand in hand with a greater workload. The new position will involve new tasks and greater responsibilities. You may have to adapt to an altogether different role if, for example, you have been member of a team and now you are the team leader. This will demand additional skills. A promotion can raise self-doubts and initially make you feel apprehensive.

Affirmations

- I am calm and collected as I turn my hand to new tasks.
- I look forward to learning new things, becoming stronger and more confident.
- I am finding it easy to adapt to my higher position and I am pleasantly surprised at how well I am coping.

Script

I deserve this promotion! Others recognise my talents and it is OK for me to do so too. Calmly and smoothly I get to grips with all the new tasks I need to learn. I am finding it easy to liaise with others, to find out what I need to know and to master any new challenges that come my way. I am open-minded and flexible and look forward to mastering new skills. I work happily and enthusiastically: my performance is very good indeed. Even when there is a lot to do, it is perfectly OK for me to take breaks. I am aware of my own worth and I look after myself. I give my best and work hard: I am successful, confident and strong.

Scenario

Imagine you could see one year into the future. You are well into your new job, carrying out all the tasks easily and efficiently. See yourself speaking confidently with colleagues and customers and imagine going home with a sense of happiness and satisfaction.

Tips and tricks

1. Be aware that whatever you don't know today you can learn tomorrow. As long as you are truly interested in what you are doing, learning will be a pleasure, enhancing your job satisfaction. If you have problems with learning, read the section 'Intellectual Skills' (*see* pages 206–9).

2. If you don't understand something, *ask*. Don't pretend to know when you don't. It is better to ask straight away than to blunder along and have to admit later that you didn't know.

3. Be prepared to give yourself six months until you start feeling comfortable in your new position. *This is normal.* There is a lot of new knowledge to absorb, so don't give yourself a hard time throughout this initial assimilation period.

4. Don't spend your higher salary all at once. Before making major decisions, such as buying a larger house, give yourself six months to settle into your new position. Making big financial commitments puts you under pressure, and this is the last thing you need when you are in the process of adapting to a new job.

5. Keep your feet on the ground. Just because you have been promoted doesn't mean you are better than others. Keep in contact with former colleagues and be friendly with the people who work for you. Your position has changed, not you.

6. Keep a sense of humour. Having been promoted should not stop you from having a good laugh every once in a while.

7. Make sure your private life is not reduced to zero. Your family and friends still need you, and you need them.

WORKING FROM HOME

Computer links have made it possible to work from home while still being in touch with the office. This has many advantages – you save money and time because you don't have to commute to and from your workplace, your working hours are more flexible and you get to see more of your children.

On the other hand, having your family around you while you are trying to work can also be a bind, especially when you have not set clear boundaries for the children about noise and other disruptions. In addition, it can be very tempting to work day and night. It is so easy to pop into the study and do 'just one more thing', and before you know it you have worked twelve hours without a break and forgotten to eat . . .

A special problem occurs when you live and work from home as a single person. Without other people around you to exchange opinions with or chat with during breaks, you can easily begin to feel isolated from the world around you. Telephone calls and e-mails are no replacement for the physical presence of other people.

Affirmations

- I am part of this world and connected in spirit with others.
- I am connecting with others easily and provide myself with opportunities to socialise with others after my work has been done.
- I look forward to meeting friends and my happy anticipation makes me work better and more efficiently.

Script

I enjoy all the advantages of working from home. I am very aware of the good this situation brings me. I am working happily and efficiently and time just flies by. Every ten minutes seem like one as I concentrate on what I am doing. While I am working, I am forgetting everything around me. When I finish my work, I start thinking about myself and what I need. I take my need for companionship seriously and make arrangements to meet up with others. I look after myself well because I deserve it. I make sure I provide myself with lots of opportunities to meet up with old and new friends, to feel the closeness of other human beings, to enjoy their presence and feel that I am part of humanity.

Scenario

Remember when you last had a good time or an enjoyable encounter with one or several friends or acquaintances. Remember this event in as much detail as you can until you feel the positive feeling of togetherness inside you.

Tips and tricks

1. Provide yourself with human contact by making arrangements in advance. When you have a party or a get-together lined up, it gives you something definite to look forward to.

2. Speaking to friends or family on the phone is OK but it is not enough. In order to counterbalance isolation, you need face-to-face conversations with someone.

3. Leave the house *at least* once a day, if possible more often, and make sure you speak to several people face to face, in shops, supermarkets, at bus stops. If you have problems with shyness, work through the 'Shyness' section first (*see* pages 155–7).

4. Evening classes are a good way of interacting with others. If you find it difficult to express yourself verbally, a dance class could be ideal for you.

GOING SELF-EMPLOYED

Over the last fifty years, whole industries, such as coal mining and shipbuilding, have nearly or completely disappeared. Other sectors, such as the IT and leisure industries, have grown explosively. Companies merge and shed employees, and while you could once rely on your job being for life, this security has gone. Many companies now cut back on expenses by outsourcing work rather than pay a full-time employee to do the job in-house. This creates opportunities for those who want to work for themselves and prefer this to being employed.

It is quite a big step to leave employment where money is coming in regularly and set up on your own. This needs to be planned very carefully as there clearly are some risks. Your business may not take off as expected, but the mortgage and bills still need to be paid. A great number of businesses don't make it past their first year of trading.

The most difficult thing at the start of being self-employed is to assess whether it is worth continuing your enterprise when not enough money has come in during the first year of trading. Clearly, you need to give a business time to develop, but how long should you allow this phase to take? It is essential to budget for the initial six to eight months to make sure you can cover your costs, even if the business is not making much money. It seems contradictory, but it is when no money is coming in to start with that you need to spend resources on advertising to generate income.

The following suggestions are for those anxiety-ridden days when you are waiting for the phone to ring or e-mails to hit your computer with enquiries for your product or services.

Affirmations
- I look forward to my business taking off.
- I deserve wealth and prosperity. The doors to abundance now open wide for me.
- I am attracting customers/clients like a big magnet.

Script
I have prepared myself thoroughly for my business venture and I am now ready to let it begin to develop. I invite prosperity and success into my life. I feel confident and strong. I believe in myself and I believe in my business and look forward to success and prosperity. Every day I have new ideas and I use them in the most positive ways to assist my business to succeed and flourish. I sleep soundly at night, I feel calm and confident during the day and use my time well to gather more information and make new contacts helpful to my business. I am outgoing and optimistic and I have a vision which I pursue with enthusiasm. The strength of my vision and my positive attitude attracts customers/clients into my life and makes me deliver an excellent service/product which I can be proud of. My standards are high, the quality of my work outstanding, and customers/clients are attracted to my business and I warmly welcome them.

Scenario

Imagine your business having taken off and you giving excellent service or delivering a superb product. See yourself with your customers/clients, see them smile happily, hear them thank you. Have an image in your mind of your bank statement showing a healthy balance.

Tips and tricks

1. The safest way of starting your own business is to stay in employment while conducting your business in the evenings or at weekends. That way you can cover the initial period where little or no money is coming in from your business. Once your venture has started taking off, you can either reduce your hours at work or let go of it altogether.

2. Plan your business thoroughly *before* starting it, especially if great financial outlay is involved. If you need a loan, your bank will want to see a business plan, but even if you can finance your new business yourself, it makes sense to put together a financial plan for yourself showing how you are going to get through the first year.

3. Do not sit by the phone and wait for it to ring! It will only make you feel downhearted and anxious. Instead, use your time by checking what else you can do to get people to contact you and give you business.

4. When you have periods where you want to give up, use the affirmation 'I give thanks for having received'. Pretend it has already happened. This way you are attracting success into your life.

5. It is not a sign of failure if you need to take up part-time work if your business does not take off as well as you hoped. You can always let it go once your business is doing better.

Sometimes, all it takes is one satisfied customer who tells all their friends about you . . .

Michaela's Story

Michaela (28) had been working as a personal assistant for many years when she noticed that she was becoming dissatisfied and bored with her professional life. She felt she could do her job with her eyes shut – there were no challenges any more. She was single and on a very good salary which afforded her a pleasant lifestyle. She wanted to maintain this but she knew she needed a change of direction.

Michaela had always been fascinated by the different scents of aromatherapy oils and she decided to train as an aromatherapist. She greatly enjoyed learning all about the oils and massage on her course. Once she had qualified, she invested in a treatment couch and started by inviting friends and family to come for treatment. She only charged them ten pounds because she felt she was still training and was not yet as efficient as an experienced aromatherapist. She was hoping that her friends would recommend her but this did not happen. Luckily, she had not given up her full-time job, so finances were not a problem.

However, the more Michaela worked with aromatherapy, the less meaningful her job as a PA became to her. She decided to investigate further what could be done. Her research led her to magazines and papers, associations and established practitioners. She looked at advertising and sharing a room with someone who already had their own practice.

She came across a reflexologist who worked at a fitness centre. Brenda was looking to share her room with someone else, as she didn't want to be there more than two of the three days the centre made her take on. This was ideal for Michaela. She started off by putting a note up on the noticeboard in the fitness centre and she also advertised regularly in the local free newspaper. She continued to subsidise her business with her full-time work for another year until she had built up enough business to dedicate herself to aromatherapy.

OUT OF THE RAT RACE

In 1901, life expectancy for men was forty-six years and fifty for women. Today, this has risen to seventy-five and eighty years respectively. This means that we spend more time working, but it also means that we have more years of life left after retirement. Pensioners have become a consumer group to be taken seriously. Generally, pensioners have more money today to spend on travelling and entertainment, and they are healthier and more active. And yet, the end of professional life, together with the gradual loss of work-related social contacts, can constitute a stressful change as a new life phase begins.

Another stressful situation is losing your job through redundancy. The trauma lies not just in the loss of income, but also in the anxieties that arise about finding new employment, especially if you are over a certain age. Companies tend to want younger employees who they can train up because they are cheaper, and this can result in older job applicants standing less chance of getting the job.

UNEMPLOYMENT

Losing your job can be a frightening experience, particularly when you have a family to support. It is essential to keep on applying for jobs, no matter how many rejections you get.

Affirmations

- The right job is already on its way to me.
- I pursue the search for a new job actively, optimistically and persistently.
- The opportunity to look for a new job turns out to my advantage. This is the best thing that could happen to me.

Script

I am now beginning to build my confidence steadily and solidly. Every day I do at least one active thing to find a new job. I feel calm and confident, stable and strong. No matter how long it takes, I continue to pursue my aim with courage and determination. I know that a well-paid and interesting job is already on its way to me; all I have to do is stay active. I do everything I possibly can to open the door to new opportunities. No matter what anyone else says, I know I can be successful. I am pleased to discover that I am inspired with a great number of good ideas and this helps me find a job which suits me in every respect. I am calm and relaxed in interviews. Success is a certainty.

Scenario
Imagine going to work in the morning and entering an office building or a factory. Picture yourself being greeted in a friendly manner by colleagues. Visualise yourself working happily throughout the day and then going home, content and fulfilled.

Tips and tricks
1. Don't be thrown by negative comments or unfavourable statistics. The employment situation may not be brilliant at the moment, but you can still find a job – not just any old job, but a job that is better than your previous one.

2. The only way you *won't* find a new job is either if you don't start looking or if you stop looking. As long as you keep looking you will eventually be successful.

3. Be flexible. Accept that you may have to move or go on a course to further your chances of a new job.

4. Make use of your time by furthering your knowledge in your field. Potential employers will be impressed by your initiative, and this could give you the edge over the other job applicants.

5. Have you really done everything to find a new job? Make sure you tell as many people as possible what you are looking for. The person you are speaking to might not be able to help, but they may know someone else who can.

6. Keep to a daily routine, even though you are not working at the moment. Get up at a reasonable time, dress properly and actively undertake something every day to find a new job.

7. Make a list of all your job-related strengths. Practise talking in front of the mirror about your strengths in a confident way. This is a good dry run for interviews.

RETIREMENT

Retirement is often associated with 'getting old' and ceasing to be a useful member of society. What is there to do now? What is going to give the day structure since the work routine is no longer in place? Those people who have always had interests outside work will fare better when it comes to retirement than those who depended on work to give meaning to their life.

Affirmations
- I can enjoy building up a new daily routine.
- I am thrilled that I can finally do exactly as I please. Life starts now!
- I am looking forward to a new start full of interesting and exciting challenges.

Script
I am looking forward to this new phase in my life. It is fun making plans and trying out new things. I can finally pursue my hobbies and interests to my heart's content. I get involved in my new life more and more deeply and this makes me happy. I can now relax and enjoy myself and make more time for my social life. I find it easy to make new friends and to stay in touch with old friends. Others are attracted by my good mood and happiness. My life is now unfolding fully and I am happy to have handed over work to my successor. I am surprised

and delighted at how fulfilled I am feeling in my new life. Every day I discover new and interesting things and I now have time to explore them further. It is a good feeling to leave the responsibilities of work behind me and live in the moment.

Scenario
Imagine conversing and laughing with new and old friends, having lively discussions and going out together.

Tips and tricks
1. If you are due to retire in a few months' time and you have not yet developed interests outside your workplace, start doing so now. Once you have started building up an interesting life independent of your work, retirement becomes a lot easier when it finally happens.

2. Be prepared for an interim period where your spouse has to adapt to you being at home, especially if they were used to having the house to themselves while you were at work. See how things go for a couple of weeks and, if necessary, sit down and discuss with your spouse any problems that may have developed through you being there all the time.

3. Allow yourself a bit of time to come to terms with your retirement. It is a big change if you no longer need to go to work every day. If you miss a daily work routine, you might want to get involved in a charitable project on a part-time basis.

4. If you have not already done so, find a hobby. It does not have to be anything useful – the main thing is that you are enjoying it. The best remedy against getting old is to keep interested in the outside world. This will also make you a more interesting person to be with.

5. If you are single or widowed, this could be the ideal time to have a pet for company. If your pet is a dog, it can also prove to be an ideal conversation opener when you are out and about. Your pet could actually help you make new friends.

Further Reading

Dr. F. Batmanghelidj, *Your Body's Many Cries for Water*, Tagman, 2000

Art Brownstein, *Healing Back Pain Naturally*, Newleaf, 2000

Adelle Davis, *Let's Get Well*, Thorsons, 1992

Kathleen Desmaisons, *Potatoes Not Prozac*, Simon & Schuster, 1999

Richard Gerber, *Vibrational Medicine*, Bear & Co, 1996

Ute Gerzabek, *The Power of Breathing*, Marshall Publishing, 1999

Marilyn Glenville, *Natural Solutions to Infertility*, Piatkus, 2000

Paul Houghton, *A Guide to Homoeopathic Remedies*, Souvenir Press, 2000

Maggie La Tourelle with Anthea Courtenay, *Principles of Kinesiology*, Thorsons, 1992

Vera Peiffer, *Positively Fearless,* Element Books, 1993

Vera Peiffer, *Positively Single*, Element Books, 1991

Vera Peiffer, *Positive Thinking*, Element Books, 1989

Vera Peiffer, *Principles of Stress Management*, Thorsons, 1996

Vera Peiffer, *Principles of Hypnotherapy*, Thorsons, 1996

Patricia Quinn, *Healing with Nutritional Therapy*, Newleaf, 1998

Jane Revell, *Success over Stress*, Saffire Press, 2000

Lynne Robinson and Helge Fisher, *The Mind Body Workout – Pilates and the Alexander Technique*, Pan, 1998

Michael Van Straten, *Foods for Mind and Body*, HarperCollins, 1997

Useful Addresses

Alexander Technique

The Society of Teachers of the Alexander Technique (STAT)
129 Camden Mews
London NW1 9AH

Tel: 020 7284 3338
E-mail: info@stat.org.uk
Website: www.stat.org.uk

Bereavement Counselling

CRUSE Bereavement Care
Cruse House
126 Sheen Road
Richmond
Surrey TW9 1UR

Tel: 0870 167 1677
Website: www.crusebereavementcare.org.uk

Educational Kinesiology

Kinesiology Federation
P.O. Box 17153
Edinburgh EH11 3WQ

Tel: 08700 113 545

Health Kinesiology

Health Kinesiology UK
Sea View House
Long Rock
Penzance TR20 8JF

Tel: 01736 719030
Website: www.healthk.co.uk

Homeopathy

British Homeopathic Association
26a Devonshire Street
London W1N 1RJ

Tel: 020 7935 2163

Hypnotherapy

The Atkinson-Ball College of Hypnotherapy and Hypno-
Healing
P.O. Box 70
Southport PR9 9HR

Tel: 01704 576 285
Website: www.abc-hypnotherapy.co.uk

Nutrition

Institute for Optimum Nutrition
Blades Court
Deodar Road
London SW15 2NU

Tel: 020 8877 9993
E-mail: info@ion.ac.uk

Pilates

Body Control Pilates Association
17 Queensbury Mews West
London SW7 2DY

Infoline: 01753 655500

Positive Thinking

The Peiffer Foundation
P.O. Box 139A
Surbiton KT6 6WE

Tel: 020 8241 1962
Website: www.vera-peiffer.com

Relationship problems/Psychosexual counselling

RELATE
Littlechurch Street
Rugby
Warks CV21 3AP

Tel: 01788 573 241
Website: www.relate.org.uk

Sexual orientation

PACE
34 Hartham Road
London N7 9JL

Tel: 020 7700 1323
E-mail: pace@dircon.co.uk
Website: www.pacehealth.org.uk

Stress Management

The Stress Management Counsellors Association
808A High Road
London N12 9QU

Tel: 020 8446 2210
E-mail: stressless@icet.net

Index

PIATKUS BOOKS

If you have enjoyed reading this book, you may be interested
in other titles published by Piatkus. These include:

All Piatkus titles are available from:

Piatkus Books Ltd, c/o Bookpost, PO Box 29, Douglas, Isle of Man, IM99 1BQ

Telephone (+44) 01624 677 237
Fax (+44) 01624 670 923
Email: bookshop@enterprise.net
Free Postage and Packing in the United Kingdom
Credit Cards accepted. All Cheques payable to Bookpost

Prices and availability are subject to change without prior notice.
Allow 14 days for delivery. When placing orders, please state if you do not
wish to receive any additional information.